the COMPLEX religion of TEENS

Other books by this author:

Maximum Marriage
Why Our Teenagers Leave the Church

To order, **call 1-800-765-6955.**

Visit us at www.reviewandherald.com
for information on other Review and Herald® products.

the COMPLEX religion of TEENS

A Lifetime of
Research Reveals
How Adolescents
Relate to
Spiritual Matters

ROGER DUDLEY

REVIEW AND HERALD® PUBLISHING ASSOCIATION
Since 1861 | www.reviewandherald.com

The Review and Herald® Publishing Association publishes biblically based materials for spiritual, physical, and mental growth and Christian discipleship.

The author assumes full responsibility for the accuracy of all facts and quotations as cited in this book.

This book was
Edited by Gerald Wheeler
Copyedited by James Cavil
Cover designed by Ron J. Pride
Interior design and electronic makeup by Heather Rogers
Typset Bembo 12/14.5

PRINTED IN U.S.A.

11 10 09 08 07   5 4 3 2 1

Library of Congress Cataloging-in-Publication Data

Dudley, Roger L.
The complex religion of teens: a lifetime of research reveals how adolescents relate to spiritual matters / Roger Dudley.
     p. cm.
ISBN 978-0-8280-2025-1
1. Seventh-day Adventist teenagers—Religious life. 2. Church work with teenagers—Seventh-day Adventists. I. Title.
BV4531.3.D83 2007286.7'320835—dc22

                              2006102810

Contents

Introduction

H. L. Mencken reportedly said,
"For every complex problem, there is a
solution that is simple, neat, and wrong."

My purpose in this book is to try to understand the religious and spiritual experience of adolescents. Since it is part of the larger teenage personality, we must also probe adolescent development in general. And it is an unbelievably complicated subject. Some friends will hear about this book and ask me to explain my findings in one sentence or one paragraph. Such a simple answer would be wrong. Adolescents are complex beings. Many factors of genetics and environment shape their behavior. We can try to find our way through the maze, but we must always do it with humility. I hope to offer some answers, but I do it tentatively, realizing I will never have the final ANSWER.

A long time ago I heard the legend of the king who sent out a number of his servants to discover the essential truth of the universe. They were to sum it up in one sentence. According to the story they came back with a number of answers, none of which could stand up to scrutiny. Finally one person found it and, of course, got to marry the king's daughter. I think the winning observation was "There's no free lunch." Or it could have been "You can't put the toothpaste back in the tube."

Both observations have merit, but I think I have a better one. After observing life, I came up with a statement that I propose covers everything. I have used it in classes through the years, and no one has ever proved it wrong. One student gave me a plaque to hang over my desk. It reads: "Dudley's theorem: Everything is more complex than it first appears." Think about it.

It is certainly true when it comes to understanding teenagers. So as we begin this journey, let us grasp the truth we find, but remember that there will always be more to learn.

My Personal Experience

So how did I get into this? Allow me to give you a brief biography, because this book is not just an academic exercise but a reflection of my whole life. My first job out of college was teaching grades 5 to 8 in a church school. Then I spent a period in pastoring. Although the latter was what I had trained for, I felt a desire to get back to teaching young people. So I took a position as principal and teacher of grades 7 to 10 in a junior academy. It was a wonderful experience as I taught, played, and fellowshipped with some really marvelous kids for three years. Ultimately it led to my appointment as principal and teacher of grades 7 and 8 in a large church school.

To my surprise, I eventually found myself elected to a position in the conference office and spent the next nine years as superintendent of education and youth ministries director (we used to call it Missionary Volunteer secretary) in two different conferences. From there I went to be principal of a large boarding academy. Then it was senior religion teacher and counselor at two different boarding academies. So I spent most of my first 28 years of service working with teenagers. By that time I was getting a little old for frontline youth service and took a call to the Christian Ministry Department of the Theological Seminary at Andrews University. Here I have been for the past 26 years. At the time of writing I have worked for the Seventh-day Adventist denomination nearly 53 years.

However, making the shift from conference and academy ministry did not mean that I had abandoned my work for teenagers. In between jobs I sandwiched time to earn a doctorate in psychology and counseling. When it came time to choose a dissertation topic, I selected "Alienation From Religion as Perceived by Students Attending Seventh-day Adventist Academies in the United States." While I had written very little in my first 24 years of service, my doctoral program helped me discover a new researching and writing ministry. I devoted this newfound talent to studying teenagers, for whom I had worked and had loved so long. My first book, *Why Teenagers Reject Religion and What to Do About It,* emerged from my dissertation and years of youth ministry.

After that I drew on my counseling experience to compose *When Teenagers Cry Help* which won a Write Now award from the Review and Herald. Next I tried to look at how adolescents relate to culture in *The World: Love It or Leave It!* Finally, I made a long study of how values get passed on from generation to generation, and authored what I consider to be my most significant book: *Passing On the Torch*. My book editor said that he considered it to be one of the two most important books he had ever edited. I also served on the committee that oversaw the original Valuegenesis project, which studied 11,000 youth in grades 6 to 12, and received the assignment of writing the report that appeared as *Valuegenesis: Faith in the Balance*.

But I really got back to direct interaction with the youth in the mideighties with the Youth Retention Study. This groundbreaking research sponsored by the North American Division randomly selected more than 1,500 young people 15 or 16 years old and surveyed them every year for 10 years. No other religious group has ever attempted such a feat. After the first year my coworker Janet Kangas and I published the results in *The World of the Adventist Teenager*. During those 10 years I exchanged scores of letters with the teenagers who became young adults, and constructed profiles of their development. At the close of the project I reported on the findings in *Why Our Teenagers Leave the Church*.

I take space to tell you all this because in order to really understand this book you have to know where I am coming from and to feel some of my passion for this subject. Next, my interest in it has involved not only direct ministry and writing but also teaching.

My friend Randy Wisbey was professor of youth ministry at the seminary. Developing a curriculum for a Master of Arts in youth ministry, he asked for my input. Even if my direct contact with young people was now more limited, I could still teach pastors and teachers how to do it. So I developed two courses for the program— Counseling Youth and Young Adults and Understanding the Religious Experience of Adolescence. I taught both courses for several years until I officially retired from teaching.

It is the latter course that is the basis for this book. However, since all of my teenage-oriented books except *Why Our Teenagers Leave the Church* are long out of print and no longer available, I have drawn some material from these works, particularly *Passing On the Torch*, to broaden the present work beyond what I covered in the course.

The bottom line, then, is that in this writing I have tried to sum up much of what I have learned about teenagers in 53 years of ministry and continuous research and study. I suspect that it will constitute my last book about the subject of teenagers. It is my final attempt to share my experience with pastors, teachers, and concerned parents as they reach out to save our youth for Christ and for the church. A new generation of leaders is picking up the torch where some of us are laying it down.

I would be remiss to fail to point out that I have had a lot of help in my research and writing ministry. My position at the seminary as director of the Institute of Church Ministry has allowed me generous time to do this research and writing. The North American Division of Seventh-day Adventists has supported my projects financially and promoted them. Esteemed colleagues have consulted with me, and, in some cases, coauthored books and articles. I am especially indebted to the dozens of students who have helped me through the years in collecting data and helping me make sense out of the results. I have named a number of them in the preface to *Why Our Teenagers Leave the Church*. My dear wife, Peggy, has been a tremendous inspiration and help throughout my career. Most of all, I thank God, who has allowed me all these wonderful years of service. I give all glory to Him.

Spiritual Teenagers: Oxymoron?

Our youth love luxury. They have bad manners, contempt for authority; they show disrespect for their elders. Children are now the tyrants, not the servants, of their households. They no longer rise when their elders enter the room. They contradict their parents, chatter before company, gobble up their food, and tyrannize teachers."

Is this a quote from the latest *Newsweek* report on the current youth scene? Hardly. Tradition has attributed the passage to Socrates, who died in 399 B.C. So what else is new? For centuries older adults have been complaining that the younger generation was "going to the dogs." "Kids nowadays are much worse than when I was young," tongues wag.

But is that true? Sure, it's easy to document that many youth are engaged in frighteningly risky behaviors, such as smoking, drinking, drugs, and sexual activity. But is there more than what we see on the surface? Let me tell you about Karen, Mini, Tim, and Alan.

Some years ago I received an invitation to be the evening speaker at the youth tent for a weeklong camp meeting. Now, it was a traditional camp meeting—out in the country, tents pitched in a meadow, attendees living in old wooden cabins and family tents. A prominent Adventist minister was scheduled to speak at both the evening meeting in the adult tent and at 11:00 in the morning in the youth tent.

My first day there I attended the morning meeting and sat down

The Complex Religion of Teens

near the back of the tent. I thought it might be well to observe in order to know what I might face that evening. Two girls in their early teens came in during the singing and sat down about three rows ahead of me. After a few minutes they got up and walked out. *H'mm,* I thought. *They stayed just long enough to report to their mothers that they had gone to the meeting; then they skipped out for other entertainment.*

But I was wrong. In a short time they returned, bringing two boys who sat on either side of them. *Well,* I thought, *the girls here are friendly.* However, as the speaker delivered his message, the four of them didn't seem to be paying much attention.

They began to pick up clumps of grass and threw them at each other. Then they started a game in which the one on the end would bump into the next one, who would pass it on to his or her neighbor, and so on until the bumps rippled back and forth across the row.

Toward the end of the sermon they all bent over toward the ground. *Perhaps they are praying,* I thought. But as the meeting ended, they got up and walked out the back. Or rather they waddled, having tied their shoelaces together. *Ooh!* I thought. *I've got a challenge here.*

After the meeting I had a conference with the young pastors in charge of the youth tent. Telling them what I had seen, I expressed some concern about what might happen at the evening service. "Don't be too quick to judge," one of them advised. "They're basically good kids."

Early the next morning there was a gathering outside in which the kids held hands in a circle and sang popular spiritual songs and then divided into small groups for prayer. I participated, and so did the four of them. When the time came for the prayer groups, I noticed that they had gone off in a group by themselves. So I went over to them and asked if I might join in their prayer session.

Before we prayed, I said, "I would like to pray for each of you, so would you please tell me your names?" That's when I got acquainted with Karen, Mini, Tim, and Alan. Each one of them prayed. Then when it came my turn, I had trouble remembering all of the names. So I prayed for Karen, Mini, *Ken,* and Alan. No sooner did I say "Amen" then they all chorused together, "His name is Tim!"

12

"I'm so sorry," I apologized. "I've just met you, and I forgot one of the names."

"Oh, that's OK," Mini responded with genuine concern. "God knew what you meant." At that moment I knew that we were going to have a good week. The girl understood something about God, and she also cared enough to spare me embarrassment. Those kids had more to them than I had figured.

Sure enough—we had a great week! The four (along with many others) participated in every daytime event. They came to all my meetings too. Evening by evening they kept moving forward, until they sat in the front row. We began to form a bond.

One evening late in the week only three showed up. "Where's Mini?" I inquired.

"She had to do something else," they explained.

"Well, how can I preach if you are not all there to support me?" I said it in a teasing manner. Unexpectedly, they got up and walked out. *Now I've offended them,* I thought. But a few minutes later they came back, dragging Mini. We were all there. The meeting could go on.

The final evening I spoke on being faithful and on seeing each other in heaven. "We'll all meet around the tree of life," I invited. Then I began to personalize the imagined gathering, mentioning different youth and what they would bring to the occasion, based on our experiences of the week. For example, the singer with the beautiful voice who would provide special music. Finally, I came to my special friends. "I know Karen, Mini, Tim, and Alan will be there because they come to everything. They'll get their heads close together. Then I'll notice something. They have tied their halos together."

The instant the meeting was over, they rushed to the platform. "You saw us that first day, didn't you?" they smiled. We all had a good laugh. The next day before I left, they came to my cabin, bringing me a homemade card. They had written some favorite Bible texts and then drawn a smiley face and scrawled: "Smile, Roger Dudley, cuz Jesus loves you! P.S. And everyone." I was glad that I didn't let those first impressions keep me from knowing some precious kids.

The Complex Religion of Teens

Over the years I have worked with young people in many capacities. I have taught in church school and two boarding academies, and been principal of a large academy. And I served as youth ministries director of two local conferences. For many years I have researched teenagers and their spiritual lives. After having associated with hundreds of them, I never fail to be amazed at the depth of spirituality in so many of those kids.

Greg was like many other academy students—not a bad fellow, not hostile, not openly rebellious, but not overtly pious, either. In the religion class that I taught he sometimes "played the devil's advocate" on some of the doctrinal and ethical issues we discussed. He was good-natured in his dissent, and I considered him my friend. But he had not impressed me as being particularly spiritual.

Then near the end of the school year the campus pastor scheduled a final Friday night Communion service. After a brief meditation in the chapel, we separated and went to the rooms designated for the foot-washing service. I held back to make sure that everyone had a partner. All seemed to be paired off and about their sacred task, but I noticed a group of three young men together. One was Greg. *Maybe they're just fooling around,* I thought, and went over to investigate. Trying to intervene tactfully, I asked, "Does one of you need a partner?"

Greg looked up and smiled. "We were going to do a threesome," he said. "But Dr. Dudley, *you* don't have a partner. Here, let me serve you."

Somewhat amazed, I sat down while Greg brought a basin of water and washed my feet. Then he paused. "Dr. Dudley, I'd like to pray with you," he offered. I nodded assent, and Greg, still kneeling at my feet, offered a simple and beautiful prayer, asking God to guide and bless me. It surprised and deeply moved me. The memory of that experience continues to refresh me spiritually.

That little incident illustrates a truth that I have seen demonstrated many times in many ways. Nearly all Adventist teenagers hold spiritual values that are important to them. To the casual onlooker they may appear as if they never had a serious thought or ever cared about anything outside of this world. Because they wish to seem avant-garde and self-possessed ("cool") to their peers, they may put on a facade of indifference to religious values.

Yet when we get close to these adolescents over a period of time, we begin to get glimpses that reveal something deeper than what has seemed apparent on the surface. Those who have seen teenagers as careless and have not realized that values are really important to them will often find themselves surprised by what they discover in those young people.

This is not the place to review that vast literature on adolescent religiosity. But researchers have continually tapped that wellspring. The growing evangelical youth movement as exemplified by such organizations as Campus Life and Youth for Christ is gaining prominence. In my own research on 1,500 teenagers I found that 63 percent claimed to pray every day, and another 16 percent at least weekly. Only 4 percent never prayed. Devotional reading is less frequent, but still nearly half (46 percent) said they read their Bibles at least weekly.

About 30 percent of this representative group indicated that they had been "growing" Christians since they were young, and 15 percent had had a "conversion experience" during a specific period. Two comments will serve as examples: "The most important thing in life to me is Jesus and having a daily walk with Him. That is also my biggest struggle. I find it too easy to wake up late and dash out the door without having morning worship. It is my toughest struggle."

"I also feel that continually learning more about God is very important, and I try to do as much of this as I can."

I think about the 30 to 60 young people at Andrews University who for years have gone every Sabbath afternoon to the nearby underprivileged city of Benton Harbor, where they visit door to door and conduct children's Bible classes. I think about two girls at Andrews University who get up early every Sabbath morning and fix a free breakfast for students who then conduct Sabbath school.

What about the hundreds of youth who serve each year as student missionaries? At an academy where I once taught, student-led prayer groups met around the flagpole for singing and prayer *every morning* for the entire school year. When I was a youth ministries director, we used to take groups of kids out on the street or to the park, where they talked to other young people about Jesus and how to have a relationship with Him. I wish you could see what scores of students have written in my academy yearbooks.

No, the younger generation is *not* going to the dogs. In spite of the new and fierce temptations they may face, I sense in them a spiritual vibrancy. They need our prayers and support, but we have reason to be encouraged. God is working.

Of course, the values of today's teenagers may be different from those we older individuals are used to. I once taught a senior religion class in an Adventist academy. It was a typical group, but one student stood out. Even his classmates considered Jerry rather weird. Fascinated by the military, he wore khaki Army surplus clothes, and once I saw him drilling some younger children with their "fake" rifles.

His home was in the community, and at Christmas season his parents invited the whole senior class to a party at their home. Since I was a class sponsor, I got to go too. It was not an organized party. The main activity was to wander through their house and help oneself to the delicious refreshments laid out in most rooms.

What a house! Jerry's parents were well-off professional people. They had collected antiques reminiscent of eighteenth-century upper-class America. Poster beds and all. I felt transported to colonial Williamsburg.

Until I came to Jerry's room. It was very stark—plain metal bed, basic furniture, and pictures of guns and other police implements plastered on the walls. It didn't look like it belonged in that house. Obviously he didn't want to be identified with the values and tastes of his parents.

In class I assigned the students to write a brief paper on their philosophy of life, including their relationship to God. Here are some excerpts from Jerry's composition:

"My relationship with God is not always what it should be. It is sometimes good and sometimes evil. It seems as if things are always going wrong. I'll admit I should improve, but right now it seems almost impossible. My philosophy of life is to keep it as long as you can. Choose the way you want to go, right or wrong, but let God help you, because you don't know how sweet and precious life is until you have faced death at least once.

"People tend to think of me as a 'war lover' or a cruel person when in actuality I sometimes find myself unable to smash a bug. I'm not always a cruel person. It's just that I have an interest in weapons and warfare. Who knows? Maybe God has a purpose for my knowledge. Maybe he wants me to help Christians escape during the time of trouble. Who knows? Everything has a purpose."

Now, I don't agree with his theology, but I have to admit that he had done some thinking about ultimate things. His values were different from mine, and probably yours, but he did have values. This is an important point that we will look at more closely in other chapters.

One method that I have often used to gain a glimpse into the inner values of young people is to get them writing. Working with a class of teenagers, I may read them a modern parable, a short personal experience, or a message poem. Then I ask them to write what meanings they have discovered and their reactions to them. And I promise that I will keep their responses confidential.

The exercise has produced amazing results. Young people who appear rebellious to faculty and parents, and who would not dare let their peers see behind the front that they have erected, often write honestly and freely about their spiritual longings. At the beginning of the semester I have asked students to write down what they wish to get out of that course. "What do you want to happen to you as a result of our spending this time together? Feel free to say anything you want," I would tell them. "You will not be judged." Reading the answers has always been a deeply moving experience.

So youth *will* choose their own values. The questions are: How can we encourage them in the process of valuing? How can we guide them in better, more principled ways of establishing values?

But if youth really do have spiritual yearnings, why do they often appear so rebellious and anti-religious? We'll turn to that topic next.

CHAPTER 2

What Makes Tommy and Tammy Tick?

Carl had been reared in a conservative Christian home. His parents were extremely careful in their religious observances. As for Carl himself, he always attended Sabbath school, church, and sometimes the prayer meeting. He didn't watch questionable television programs or go to places of worldly amusement. Always dressing appropriately, he took part in the youth meetings and participated in various service projects. The young man was so courteous that other parents considered him a model boy and wished their sons were more like him. Proudly his mother could say, "He's never given us a day's worry."

But all of a sudden in his late teens things seemed to cave in. He stopped going to church, ran around with a rough crowd, and engaged in a number of risky behaviors. Why did it happen? What changes take place in adolescents that turn some of them from sweet, cooperative youth into full-fledged rebels? Why do kids take up drugs, get involved in sex, immerse themselves in rock music or race cars, join gangs, flout rules, break their parents' hearts, and cause their teachers to shake their heads in sorrow?

The Role of Perceptions

In seeking answers to these questions, we need to look at this problem through the eyes of an adolescent rather than an adult, a view of human behavior called perceptual psychology. Arthur

Combs, Donald Avila, and William Purkey define it as follows:

"Briefly, perceptual psychology takes the position that all behavior is a function of the perceptions existing for any individual at the moment of his behaving, especially those perceptions he has of himself and of the world in which he is operating. Each of us does at every moment what seems appropriate at that instance. When the nature of perceptions is understood, even the weirdest behavior becomes comprehensible."[1]

Of course, individuals cannot usually give logical explanations for their behavior. If you ask the child why he misbehaved in class or the recent high school graduate why she broke all the rules at homecoming, neither one could probably tell you. It is because a person's perceptual field is very complex. Individuals will have varying degrees of awareness of each area of perception and are usually not able to explain how they combined to make any particular action seem to be the thing to do at a particular moment.

As a result it is usually pointless to ask adolescents why they did some wrong act. They will answer with a shrug or an "I dunno." If we press them, they will invent some reason they think will satisfy us. Yet a careful study of human behavior in general and of the background of particular cases will often help us deduce the reasons people behave the way they do. And to understand these reasons is the first step in changing behavior.

Christ was a master psychologist. "Jesus . . . knew all people and needed no one to testify about anyone; for he himself knew what was in everyone" (John 2:24, 25, NRSV). While our insights will certainly never equal those of Jesus, we can seek to emulate His understandings.

Ellen White is particularly helpful here. "It is true of men and women, and how much more of youth and children, that only as we come in touch through sympathy can we understand them; and we need to understand in order most effectively to benefit" (*Education*, p. 212). If we unpack this statement in reverse order, we get this formula: 1. We want to benefit our children and youth. 2. In order to do this, we need to understand them. 3. To understand, we must come in touch with sympathy. That's what we will try to do in this book.

The Complex Religion of Teens

Developmental Stages

It is very difficult to identify *the* cause of any human behavior because so many different things influence everything that we do. Our heredity, our environment, and our past experiences all intertwine in ways that are difficult to untangle. So in trying to understand teenagers we must not oversimplify but must approach the subject with humility. Nevertheless, we can construct an overall framework by studying developmental psychology.

Each individual goes through life by a series of stages. Everyone follows them in a predetermined order. How many stages that involves depends somewhat on a particular scholar's way of arranging them. For example, Erik Erikson has formulated eight stages: infancy, toddlers, preschool, elementary school, adolescence, early adulthood, middle adulthood, and later maturity. (I like the gentle euphemistic touch in describing that eighth stage. Harsher characterizations would have been possible.) Each stage has implications for physical, mental, emotional, and moral development.

Now, developmental psychology holds that each stage of human development seeks to accomplish certain tasks. To at least some degree, the mastery of these developmental tasks is necessary to reach maturity for that particular stage and to prepare individuals to cope with the next step in their overall growth. The important thing here is that God has programmed us so that we are driven to attempt a particular goal at the proper stage in our development. It is natural.

For example, two of the important tasks of infancy—say the first year or so—are learning to walk and to talk. When our daughter was about that stage we loved to stand her up with a few feet between the two of us and encourage her to make the journey. "Come to Daddy, dear." When she took those first few halting steps and fell into our arms, we exclaimed with glee, "She walked today," and proudly told our families about it. But the truth is that you don't have to give your child walking lessons. Their inner programming compels infants to walk. They will crawl on the floor, pull themselves up on the furniture, and finally take steps. The only way you could keep a normal kid from walking would be to tie him or her down. Can you imagine going to visit someone and seeing their 15-year-old son crawling on the floor. "Archie," I ask him, "what are you doing down there?"

"As I was growing up," he replies, "my parents were very busy in their professions. They didn't have time to teach me to walk."

Of course, it is possible that some children do not learn to walk. An accident or a disease may leave them with a disability. But if that happens, the development is not normal. Children who do not gain competence in such basic skills will be ill-prepared for the many complex tasks that await them in middle and later childhood.

The Tasks of Adolescence

We, however, will focus on adolescence. The adolescent has many important things to accomplish, including those relating to sexual development and learning the responsible behaviors that allow for economic independence in the next stage. One of the primary tasks is achieving emotional independence from parents and other adults. Some have labeled adolescence "the search for identity." The key question is Who am I? All this involves searching for meaningful self-consciousness, planning for the future, and developing a philosophy of life and values. Achieving all this is the road to mature and responsible adulthood.

However, just like the infant who never learns to walk, some adolescents fail to master their tasks. They may become emotional children in grown-up bodies. We all know adults in their 20s, 30s, and 40s who can't hold a job or make a relationship work, and who are dependent financially and emotionally on their parents.

Adolescence is a time of tremendous import. Think of what is involved. Until then children have been largely dependent upon their parents. Adults have made the major decisions for them. They have needed the constant advice of their mother and father, as well as their parents' emotional and financial support, and have lived by the rules and values of their parents' home. Preadolescents cannot conceive of operating apart from their parents.

But now all of this is going to change. Turning into adults, they will have to learn to make their own decisions. They must determine for themselves the values by which they will live. No longer merely extensions of their parents, they will become their own persons.

But achieving such independence or emancipation is a gradual process. If a child could go to bed one night and wake up the next morning as an adult, it would solve many of the concerns of teenagers. However, it doesn't happen that way. Slowly, sometimes going forward and sometimes slipping back, teenagers attempt to put the necessary emotional distance between themselves and their parents and other authority figures.

I like to think of the process as journeying through an unfamiliar swamp. A child enters at one side, and an adult emerges on the other. Getting through the swamp is tricky. Much of it will not support a person's weight. While there are solid places for the feet, they are not always evident. So the traveler gingerly seeks a stable footing. Sometimes it works, and forward progress is made. But in other cases, the traveler cannot find a way to advance, and must retreat to safe ground and try another direction. The path is ill-defined, and negotiated only by picking one's way with difficulty. Nor does the journey have a generally agreed-upon timetable. Each family is on its own.

Prolonging Adolescence

Furthermore, the prolongation of adolescence in modern Western societies has greatly complicated the process. During a large share of the world's history and in simpler cultures even today, young people could be socialized largely by their own parents in their own homes. Boys learned adult male roles and agricultural, pastoral, or small business skills by working with their fathers. Girls acquired adult female roles (mostly homemaking skills) from their mothers. By the time of puberty, adolescents knew how to take over those roles and assume their place in adult society. Society valued teenagers as essential to the family economic and social fabric. The adolescent had a sense of responsibility and career certainty that resulted in feelings of independence and clearness of identity. Quickly achieving the tasks of adolescence, such youth often married early and began families.

Today in the Western world (and perhaps as Western influence spreads to other societies) becoming an adult is not so simple. While the home remains an important factor, it must share the task of socialization with many other influences: educational institutions, peers, the media, etc. Most boys do not follow their father's occupation, and girls increasingly opt for careers outside the home. Vocational choices are varied and complicated, often requiring years of formal schooling to pursue many of them. Once society considered the "three R's" as sufficient, but then it became high school, next college, and today often graduate school. It takes a good education to get anywhere today. Many young adults remain on the dole well into their 20s.

The explosion of information bombards youth on every side. Society is in a state of rapid change. Learning quickly becomes obsolete, so the successful adult of today must acquire the skills to cope with a rapidly changing environment. The modern world has widely revised even the expectations of marriage and parenthood, calling for a maturity and command of interpersonal skills not needed in the traditional home of yesterday, where culture largely mandated its specific structure. The long transition period between being grown-up in some ways and not-yet-grown-up in others causes strain and makes it increasingly difficult for teenagers to master the necessary tasks and find their separate identity.

Consider the situation. Teenagers reach physical and sexual maturity as early as ever—perhaps even sooner because of better diets. But they are still dependent on their parents for financial support, are not yet ready for an adult career, and do not have the maturity to marry successfully and establish a home.

So here now is a physically and sexually mature adolescent driven by God-instilled forces to become a responsible, independent adult. The proper time for this in the developmental scheme of human development has arrived. The teenager has been programmed to tackle these tasks just as the infant has been programmed to walk and talk. But in most cases such individuals cannot yet assume the responsibilities of adulthood, for they still lack sufficient emotional maturity and still depend on their parents for financial support.

The Complex Religion of Teens

The Struggle for Emancipation

So what do teenagers do? They tend to relieve the tension by seeking subconsciously to make some other statement of independence. It involves differentiating themselves from their parents in some way or other. One of the easiest ways to do so is to reject some parental values. Modern society provides countless opportunities to do it: spiked hair, smoking, fast driving, drugs, pierced body parts, language, music, etc. Such a rejection is the adolescent's effective way of saying, "See, I am not the same as you. I am a different person. I can choose my own way of life."

Such psychological distancing and separation may well involve religion. If the parents are committed to a religious pattern of life, what better way for the teenager to make the break than to reject those spiritual observances! They may stop going to church, mock more pious youth, or violate behavioral standards. Psychologists are well familiar with these phenomena that David Ausubel has labeled "adolescent heresy."

Not all adolescents go through a period of open rebellion. Actually, sometimes the separation takes a positive direction, as when young people are more religious than their parents, joining witnessing groups that attempt to shake the church out of its spiritual lethargy. They may seek to become more proficient than their parents at some important task. With some the mild nonconformity is hardly noticeable on the outside but involves the way they think. But all must discover some way of establishing their independence as human beings with separate identities or they have failed the major tasks of adolescence and are doomed to a crippled adulthood.

To find an independent existence, however, is a scary experience. Leaving the nest always involves apprehension. Gay Miller, of Biola University, describes how as a sophomore college student he was trying to make his own way but didn't know where to get the money for tuition, room, and board.

"I knew that God could supply my need, but I had never been faced with this type of deadline. The burden was heavy to bear, and anxiety became my constant companion. I was also struggling with the normal and customary events that bring one through childhood into adulthood. I wanted to grow up and launch out on my own, independent of my parents. But that desire demanded a level of personal responsibility that was overwhelming. I wondered, 'Is this what it is like to be an adult?' The answer was clear: 'Yes, it is what you wanted. Now deal with it.' "[2]

A common way that teenagers deal with this is to find peer support from others going through the same stage of life. The peer group aids one to "test the waters." That is why any attempt to help teenagers develop that insists that they reject their peers is doomed to failure. Youth ministry must be to groups rather than individuals. Of course, this may involve a dependence and conformity equal to that from which they are seeking emancipation. But I like to think that the support of peers forms a useful halfway station on the journey from childhood to adulthood. After the young adult has made the passage successfully and settled the identity question, the young adult's need for peer approval diminishes. Thus the breech between parents and teenagers often heals, as the young adult no longer has to struggle for identity.

There are, however, still other factors in a developmental approach that help explain the adolescent experience. One is the changing cognitive structure—the way teenagers think. We'll look at this later in chapter 4.

---

[1] Arthur Combs, Donald Avila, and William Purkey, *Helping Relationships: Basic Concepts for the Helping Profession* (Boston: Allyn and Bacon, 1971), p. 24.

[2] *College Faith 2*, ed. Ronald Alan Knott (Berrien Springs, Mich.: Andrews University Press, 2004), p. 127.

The Religion of American Teenagers

I was a Christian for a long time," claimed 16-year-old Joy, "but right now I just—I don't believe in nothing right now. I was baptized and pretty much led a Christian life up until ninth grade, when I started doing all that stuff."

On the other hand, the deeply religious Kristen reported, "I'm just a Christian, that's it. . . . I believe that Jesus is God's Son and that He came and He died for me."

Certainly, adolescents exhibit a wide diversity of religious experience. The best overall picture of American teenage spirituality comes from the recent National Study of Youth and Religion (NSYR). Between July of 2002 and March of 2003 researchers employed a national random-digit-dial telephone survey of 3,290 teenagers between the ages of 13 and 17 and their parents. Following it, 17 project researchers conducted 267 in-depth, face-to-face interviews with a subsample of the respondents in 45 different states. A report of the massive project appears in the book *Soul Searching: The Religious and Spiritual Lives of American Teenagers,* by Christian Smith, of the University of North Carolina (with his graduate assistant Melinda Lundquist Denton, the project manager). The book is a 2005 publication of the Oxford University Press. I have drawn the information in this chapter from this work, including the statements of Joy and Kristen above, which are fragments of the reports of extensive interviews. Page numbers refer to facts taken from *Soul Searching*.

While most of the empirical research cited in my book was conducted on Seventh-day Adventist young people, I thought it appropriate to dedicate one chapter to looking at the larger American scene. After all, Adventist adolescents tend to reflect the wider culture of which they are a part. I'll start by giving a brief summary of some overarching themes that Smith and Denton introduced in more detail on pages 26-28 of their book.

General Themes

1. No one characterization of American adolescents can be completely accurate, since there is such a wide range of spiritual experiences, as illustrated in the stories of Joy (p. 13) and Kristen (p. 19).
2. A significant number of teenagers do find religion and spiritual matters to be important in their lives.
3. Among the more religious teenagers, their faith is not simply a matter of identity, but they actively practice their religion both in private devotional life and in public or corporative behaviors.
4. In spite of some general perceptions, most adolescents are not "spiritual seekers." They do not consider themselves "spiritual but not religious."
5. While many teens are intelligent about their faith, a significant number are inarticulate and confused over what they really believe.
6. Many factors compete for attention in the lives of contemporary adolescents. In an attempt to find balance, teenagers try to overlap religious activities with other areas, such as family, school, social events, friendships, etc.
7. In spite of outside influences, parents and other adults still continue to have a great effect on the religious choices of youth, either for good or for ill.
8. Adolescents who consider religion important tend to perform better and to have more success in other areas of their lives.

The Complex Religion of Teens

Religious Affiliations

About 75 percent of those 13 to 17 years of age claimed to be Christians. Of these, 23 percent were Catholic and 52 percent were distributed among the various Protestant denominations. Other faiths were represented by only tiny percentages, and only 16 percent reported that they were not religious at all. Only 0.3 percent found themselves attracted to alternative forms of religion, such as paganism or Wicca (p. 31).

Of the Protestant group, the largest denomination was Baptist (17.3 percent), followed by Methodist (4.7 percent) and Lutheran (3.5 percent), while another 13 percent identified themselves only as Christian. Seventh-day Adventist youth comprised less than half of 1 percent (0.43 percent) of the sample (p. 33).

It has often been noted that adolescents tend to rebel against the religion of their parents. Yet in this study 78 percent said that their religious beliefs were very or somewhat similar to those of their mothers and 72 percent that their religious beliefs were very or somewhat similar to those of their fathers (p. 35). As noted in theme 7 above, in spite of many other factors parental influences on adolescents are still strong.

Active or Passive

Obviously, identifying with a faith group is not synonymous with actively participating in it. But 40 percent of the sample claimed to attend religious services at least once a week. Among conservative Protestants the figure was 55 percent. Another 19 percent went one to three times a month, and 22 percent did go, but less frequently than monthly. Only 18 percent never participated in religious services (p. 37).

Nearly half (45 percent) attend religious services with *both* parents. Another 21 percent accompany either the mother or the father, and 10 percent go to religious services without either parent (p. 37). Some have questioned whether or not teen attendance is so high because parents compel them. But when asked if it were totally up to them, only 13 percent stated that they would never go. The study provided no evidence that significant numbers of adolescents would like to stop attending religious services and are only participating because their parents force them to (pp. 37, 38).

The Faith of American Teenagers

Does faith play much of a part in the experience of American adolescents? Well, half (51 percent) claimed that religious faith was extremely or very important in shaping their daily lives. Another 31 percent saw it as somewhat important, while the remaining 18 percent dismissed it as not very important or not important at all (p. 40).

Does this importance imply a relationship with God? About a third claimed they felt very close or extremely close to God. Another third were rather neutral, saying that they were either somewhat close or somewhat distant from God. The final third were very or extremely distant, with 3 percent indicating that they do not believe in God at all (p. 40). Of the total group, 84 percent said they believe in God. Another 13 percent were not sure whether or not God did exist (p. 41).

Nearly half had no doubts about their religious beliefs. Another third had a few doubts, while about a fifth had some or many doubts (p. 40). Generally the teenagers surveyed were a believing group.

But the young people had different concepts as to who or what God is. Not all who acknowledged a higher being believed in the same deity. Two thirds of the group viewed God as a personal being who involves Himself in the lives of people today. Another 13 percent assumed that God created the world but has no interaction with it or its inhabitants today—the deist view. About 14 percent saw God as not personal but something like a cosmic life force. As noted above, 3 percent did not believe in God at all, while 5 percent simply didn't know (p. 41).

The survey also addressed other areas of religious belief. For example, 63 percent definitely believed in angels, while 29 percent said "maybe." Other areas of "definitely believe" involved divine miracles, 61 percent; life after death, 49 percent; and demons or evil spirits, 41 percent. It is evident that significant numbers of adolescents are quite traditional in their religious understandings. In each of these cases approximately a third were not sure about how to answer the question, with smaller numbers who do not believe in the

The Complex Religion of Teens

specific topic at all. The largest area of nonbelief dealt with demons or evil spirits (25 percent) (p. 43).

Faith has not only a belief but an experiential dimension. More than half (55 percent) stated that they had made a personal commitment to live their lives for God. Also, 51 percent claim to have had an experience of spiritual worship that was very moving and powerful. Half of the teens have encountered what they felt were definite answers to a prayer or received specific guidance from God, and 46 percent reported that they witnessed or experienced what they believed was a miracle from God (p. 45).

Personal Religious Practices

Religion involves not only belief and experience but also some type of practices—things the faithful *do*. The percentages of adolescents who participate in various spiritual activities are as follows (p. 46):

	Total group	Conservative Protestant
Been part of a Scripture study or prayer group	27	42
Taught a Sunday school or religious education class	20	28
Fasted or denied self as a spiritual discipline	24	22
Read a devotional or religious book other than Scripture	30	45
Shared their faith with someone not of their faith	43	56
Practiced a weekly day of rest or Sabbath	31	40

In addition, nearly 40 percent said that they pray at least once a day, and more than another fourth pray at least weekly. While 20 percent pray more sporadically, only 15 percent said that they never pray.

Christian religions generally have some method by which young people make a public affirmation of their faith, such as baptism, confirmation, etc. Of the *Christian* adolescents in the sample, 46 percent had been confirmed or baptized as a public affirmation of faith. This does not include infant baptism. Among conservative Protestants the figure was 54 percent.

Adolescents tend to be group-oriented. Of the total sample, 38 percent were currently involved in a religious youth group, a figure that rises to 56 percent for conservative Protestants (p. 51). Opportunity for peer association also exists in the Sunday (Sabbath) school classes. About 36 percent claimed to attend them almost every week. More than half of the conservative Protestants do. Another third participate occasionally. But 29 percent said they never frequent such religious education classes (p. 53).

The Climate of Congregations

As the 10-year youth retention study that I conducted revealed,[*] attitudes toward their religious heritage, whether positive or negative, are greatly influenced by the climate and acceptance of their congregations. In the NSYR 79 percent of the teens reported that they had adults, other than family members, in the congregation with whom they enjoyed talking and who gave lots of encouragement (p. 60).

A most encouraging sign is that 75 percent found their own congregations to be usually a warm and welcoming place for teens. Only 5 percent said "rarely" or "never." Nearly nine out of 10 agreed that the congregation is a place that usually or sometimes makes them think. Later in this book we will discuss the importance of the "thinking climate." On the other hand, about half found the congregation to be usually or sometimes boring (p. 62).

Approximately 70 percent rated their congregations as very or fairly good places to talk about serious issues, problems, and troubles. According to 60 percent of the sample, congregations do an excellent or fairly good job of teaching those things that adolescents want to know about their own religion. What about the future? An impressive 77 percent said that when they are 25 years old they expect to be part of a congregation similar to the one they presently attend (p. 66).

The Complex Religion of Teens

Religious Types

Soul Searching classifies its subjects into three groups: spiritual seekers, disengaged, and religiously devoted. Let's look briefly at each category.

A measure of *spiritual seekers* is that they do not necessarily embrace institutional religion. When asked if believers must be involved in a religious congregation to be truly religious, 67 percent disagreed (p. 74). However, in contrast, only 8 percent said that was very true, and 46 percent replied that it was somewhat true that they were spiritual but not religious. And 43 percent said it was not true at all. So the evidence is divided (p. 78). But most teens were unfamiliar with the phrase "spiritual but not religious," so the survey offers scant support that teenagers tend to be just spiritual seekers. Most are rather traditional.

About 18 percent of adolescents labeled themselves as not religious—the *disengaged*. Even of them, only small portions saw themselves as atheists or agnostics. Most were just nonreligious or didn't know what they were (p. 86).

Some of the reasons youth raised in religious homes become nonreligious are as follows (p. 89):

	Percent
Intellectual skepticism	32
Don't know	22
Lack of interest	13
Just stopped attending	12
Disruption and troubles	10
Dislike religion	7

Factors that lead young people to become nonreligious include: parents don't attend church; parents are divorced; parents just don't understand this age group; teens don't enjoy attending services; no friends at church; negative peer group; teens belong to fewer organizations (pp. 91, 92).

One case cited in the study offers us some general insights. "Steve finds himself in the common, intellectually sticky position of many of his teenage and adult contemporaries: asserting high moral standards (e.g., belief in human rights, equality, dignity of life) while possessing few coherent, rational grounds for explaining, justifying, and defending those standards" (p. 96).

However, the lives of even nonreligious teens often contain some religious interests and values. They are not necessarily antireligious. While 18 percent never attend religious services, 43 percent of them still think of themselves as part of a religion, denomination, or church (p. 104).

Of those who don't attend services, 41 percent could give no reason, 17 percent expressed disinterest, 6 percent had suffered a bad experience in their congregation or group, and only 11 percent gave disbelief as a reason (p. 105).

But what about the *religiously devoted*? Some things that correlate with those who go to religious services regularly include: having parents for whom faith is important and who attend regularly; having positive relationships with their parents; having better educated parents; being involved in clubs, hobbies, sports, or other organized activities; having friends who are a positive influence; having close friends involved in religious groups; and rating faith as important to them (pp. 106, 107).

We may conclude that the religion of teenagers in general exhibits the following characteristics (pp. 115-117):

1. The majority of adolescents are inclusive, pluralistic, and individualistic in their religious choices.
2. Very few teenagers consider themselves to be "spiritual but not religious."
3. Parents and congregational leaders play an important role in shaping the religious experience of adolescents.
4. Peer-group friendships are key to the participation of teenagers in religious activities.
5. Teenagers who are active in a broad range of other social activities are more likely to participate in religious activities.
6. Many religiously disengaged adolescents can't explain the reasons for their lack of participation. They have simply drifted away.

---

* See Roger L. Dudley, *Why Our Teenagers Leave the Church* (Hagerstown, Md.: Review and Herald Pub. Assn., 2000).

Growing an Adolescent

Years ago I read a news story about a man who had married a 16-year-old girl and then complained that she acted like a child. Unfortunately, we sometimes do that with adolescents. We criticize them because they behave like . . . well, teenagers. We expect them to have the maturity of adults. In *My Fair Lady* Henry Higgins sings a song that asks, "Why can't a woman be more like a man?"

Often we reason that way about teenagers. Why can't they be more mature? Why can't they be more serious about spiritual and moral values? Why can't teenagers be more like us?

But it doesn't work that way. No matter how sweet, innocent, and loving little children are, they are not able to have the mature Christian experience of adults. Religion is not the same thing in children that it is in grown-ups—or in teenagers.

Cognitive Development

In chapter 2 I noted that we can explain much adolescent reaction to religion by a study of developmental stages and the tasks demanded of each stage. Here I want to take this further, but rather than talk about the tasks, I want to focus on the cognitive abilities required for spiritual development. Because most research has dealt with moral reasoning, I will treat spirituality and morality as synonyms for the purposes of our discussion.

We generally define a moral act as one based on conscious prior judgment of its rightness or wrongness. That is, advancement in spiritual maturity is not simply better behavior, but the reasoning behind that behavior. Thus a small child may do right things because of parental training but have no comprehension about why those actions are appropriate.

So, as we will see, it will be necessary to study cognitive stages in order to understand moral stages, because thinking is the source of all truly principled action. The only way we can communicate with God is through the brain. It is obvious that just as children pass through a number of predictable physical steps in their life spans, so they also advance through a series of mental or intellectual or cognitive ones. No matter how much intelligence children may have at birth, they cannot learn to do calculus in the early years. Their brains simply aren't matured enough yet. And the same principle applies in the area of morality and religion.

Developmental psychologists tell us that the stages are *sequential* and *invariant*. *Sequential* because they always follow the same order. You don't get C before B. *Invariant* because an individual must pass through each step before getting to the next one. No skipping.

Cognitive development requires *organization*—the ability to arrange and structure ideas. It calls for *adaptation*—the ability to assimilate new information into existing mental frameworks or concepts. Human beings actively construct their own understandings, but it takes time and practice. Adolescents especially must balance childhood training with new ideas. They face the challenging task of questioning and reformulating previous beliefs and ideas as their growing awareness expands their horizons. Teenagers have to make sense of the world they apprehend. The "faith crisis" of adolescence is at least partly the result of cognitive development.

One of the first proposals for stages of cognitive development came from the Swiss psychologist Jean Piaget. Piaget put questions of varying levels of difficulty to hundreds of children. He concluded that little children mostly respond to their surroundings and do not actually engage in reasoning. By about 6 years the child is able to do concrete mental operations. An example is the process of *conservation*. If one pours, in the presence of small children, two glasses with equal amounts of water into two different-sized vessels—a tall, thin one and a short, wide one—the children will pick the tall one as having more water. Only with the ability to do concrete mental operations can they see that changing the shape of an object does not affect its volume.

But such thinking is still concrete. While some children develop faster than others, Piaget felt that at about 11 years they began to be able to do abstract or formal operational thinking. Instead of seeing only one way to do something, they can weigh possibilities and choose from a number of alternatives. In addition, they can look at things from the point of view of others, and they can visualize things that are not physically present.

Not wanting to diverge into cognitive development further, I have introduced it only because it is foundational to moral and spiritual development—that which helps us in understanding adolescent spirituality. The crucial test of mature religion is the ability to abstract. God is an abstract concept—we cannot see Him, feel Him, or hear Him. Most religious concepts are abstract: faith, grace, hope, love, salvation, etc. The only way we can begin to understand any of them is through our brains. So those brains must achieve the advanced state of abstract thinking.

Stages of Moral Reasoning

Piaget saw that moral reasoning was dependent upon intellectual development. That is, justice, integrity, altruism, fairness, responsibility, and the ability to grasp another's point of view—qualities so necessary to moral reasoning—all require abstract thinking. He suggested that children pass through a series of moral stages parallel to the intellectual stages. Thus he proposed an amoral first few years, followed by the stages of *heteronomous* (other-directed) morality and *autonomous* (internalized) morality. The idea here is that in the concrete stage of thinking, standards of right and motivation to follow them come largely from outside the individual—from parents, teachers, religious leaders, etc.

However, as cognitive abilities develop, standards and motivation begin to internalize. The individual figures out the right thing to do, using various criteria, and desires to do it without pressure from outside. Self-control replaces control by others. A person is no longer motivated by fear of what people or supernatural forces might do. Internalized behavior can be based on positive attitudes toward an absent reference figure (I admire my father's honesty and want to be like him), but not on fear of punishment from that figure.

Please note that while moral reasoning cannot advance without corresponding cognitive development, the reverse is not true. Brilliant thinkers can be immoral persons by not choosing to follow the moral reasoning they are capable of. Also, age alone does not guarantee advanced cognitive development. Certain adults remain at the concrete operational stage all their lives. Some wit has joked: "A few people are thinkers; a larger number think they are thinkers; and the majority would rather die than think."

Piaget believed that up to about 10 years of age the child remained in the stage of *heteronomous* morality, or the "morality of constraint." He characterized this stage as follows:

1. One must obey rules because they are intrinsically sacred just by being rules. Rules are fixed and cannot be changed. For example, one time I was driving with an elderly passenger. Needing to turn around, I sought a suitable place. We came to an open gate that led into the large parking lot of a business. A sign on the gate declared: "NO TRESPASSING!" When I pulled in, my guest became frantic. "Didn't you see that sign? We could be arrested!" I tried to explain that what I was doing was not what the company was concerned about. We were not trespassing—only turning around. But to no avail. In the other man's mind one had to obey the sign. Don't try to reason.

2. Behaviors are totally right or totally wrong without any gray areas. Moral life is uncomplicated. The particular situation cannot determine right or wrong actions. People operating on this level have no regard for context.

3. The magnitude of the consequences determines the rightness or wrongness of an act. When told the story of two boys, one of whom dropped a whole stack of dishes while helping his mother clean up and the other who broke a single plate while reaching for a forbidden cookie, children in this stage will say the first boy is the naughtier because he broke more dishes. Humans at this stage are not able to consider motives—only behaviors and outcomes.

4. If someone gets punished for an act, the behavior must have been wrong or bad, or it wouldn't have called down punishment. Since morality in this stage is based on authority, such authority must always be right.

5. Any misfortunes that follow the violation of a rule must be direct punishments. In the case of a religious family, they are divine punishments.

To illustrate point 5: When I was 10 years old, and obviously in the heteronomous stage, an aunt who lived locally went for a long weekend to visit relatives in New York City and invited me to go along. I was excited for two reasons. First, because her daughter Joan, a cousin my age, was a favorite playmate whenever she and Aunt Pauline spent the summer each year in our town. Second, as a small-town boy I had never been to a big city. And New York! I almost bumped into people as I stared at the skyscrapers.

As we met the family at the bus, Joan pulled me aside and excitedly announced that her parents had purchased tickets for all of us to attend the circus—on Saturday. Now, while my family had Adventist roots, my parents and I had been baptized only about two months previously. I knew I shouldn't go to the circus on Sabbath, but as the only Adventist in the group I didn't know how to tell them. They were doing something special for me, and I was just a kid—so I went along with much trepidation. Because my conscience bothered me greatly, I couldn't really enjoy the show. That night I woke up violently sick to my stomach and made quite a mess. I was certain that God was punishing me for my disobedience. More mature reflection tells me that it was my digestive system upset with guilt combined with the circus hot dogs I had forced down myself during the entertainment.

Autonomous Morality

From about 11 years on up, according to Piaget, children enter the stage of autonomous morality, or "reciprocity." They begin to adopt a series of new perspectives:

1. Rules are established and maintained through reciprocal social agreement and thus are subject to modification in response to human needs or other situational demands. For example, in a marriage most roles are not fixed by gender; they must be negotiated according to the needs and gifts of the husband and wife.

2. Diversity in views of right and wrong, rather than a rigid black-and-white perspective, is seen as possible. Everything is more complicated than it first appears. Since we never know the whole truth about anything, humility in making judgments becomes part of our thinking patterns.

3. Right and wrong are determined not simply by the consequences of an act but by the motives and intentions behind it. Thus coveting, because it is an internal state, becomes the sin that underlies the breaking of all the other commandments. Jesus dealt with this at length in the Sermon on the Mount (Matt. 5).

4. Punishment is not impersonally ordained by either God or the forces of the universe. Natural consequences tend to explain the results of actions. The wayward boy did not fall through the ice as punishment from God for disobeying his mother, but because the ice was too weak to bear his weight.

5. Duty and obligation are no longer mere obedience to authority. The youth internalizes a set of principles that guide behavior. The adolescent can begin to anticipate the consequences of a course of action. Above all, children learn to put themselves in the place of other people and to realize how their actions will affect those people. From a Christian viewpoint we would want to include the principles found in God's Word as the most important guide to daily decisions.

Numerous studies have shown these stages to be positively related to age. That is, we cannot expect young people to reason morally at a higher level than their chronological maturity. However, this is not automatic. Just because teenagers have reached the age of abstract thinking does not mean that they will adopt autonomous stage moral thinking. Though it becomes cognitively possible, many adults never reason beyond the heteronomous stage.

Encouraging the Process

So how can we help adolescents develop more mature moral thinking? It comes through interaction with others—parents and peers who have already advanced to a higher level. Here are steps to use with children that can prepare them for adolescence.

1. Let the child share in making decisions in the home and school and thus gain a more comprehensive conception of rules. They come to see that rules are not simply dropped down from above but are socially constructed to the best good of the players in the game of life. Adolescents take a steadily advancing role in building their own life space.

2. Help the child take alternate and reciprocal roles with others. The key is to be able to get outside of one's immediate situation and see things from a wider perspective, including the viewpoints of others. Teenagers need to be in guided circumstances that will encourage them to do this: "So in everything, do to others what you would have them do to you, for this sums up the Law and the Prophets" (Matt. 7:12, NIV).

3. The child (and later the teenager) should be taught by both example and discussion to judge behavior by intentions rather than simply by outward actions.

As youth grow and mature, they encounter experiences for which their previous modes of thinking are inadequate. Thus the need to reorganize thinking patterns to make sense of the new information. When this restructuring takes place, it allows them to rise to a higher level of moral reasoning. So it is important to expose teenagers to a variety of experiences that will challenge their present method of dealing with reality, creating what psychologists call *cognitive dissonance*. The act of alleviating this dissonance pushes one toward further growth.*

In this book we are trying to comprehend adolescent spirituality. Understanding the cognitive and moral stages through which individuals must pass enables us to fathom better the difficulties teenagers face and to empathize with their challenges and crises. But there is more to this moral-stage business. We'll turn to that in the next chapter.

---

*See Jack R. Fraenkel, *How to Teach About Values* (Englewood Cliffs, N.J.: Prentice-Hall, 1977).

CHAPTER 5

All the World's a Stage

During the autumn of 1982 the religion editor of the New York *Times* visited the campus of Andrews University and interviewed faculty and students about the beliefs of Seventh-day Adventists. Reflecting on the visit in the October 13 issue, the editor of the *Student Movement* wrote in part:

"I haven't always been the most daring or explosive in my theology. Very often I was caught in what I was taught to believe. With him sitting in the office I began to explore some of my personal limits as an independent-thinking Christian. I decided I was a Christian, but what I hadn't decided was if I was willing to risk the traditional for the personal attitude of searching for the whys of my belief. Had I ever risked anything at all? . . .

"When he left, I stopped to think. It was then I realized the importance of using our decision-making faculties to their maximum capacity. Sometimes we become so mechanical in nature, we expect to be told what we should believe. As children it was necessary to be guided, even tugged, in the proper direction. This usually continues into adolescence, but somewhere along the line the mindless following should stop. . . .

"Just because a student has become an independent thinker, looking for answers further than his teachers or papers does not necessarily tag him as a revolutionary. He is but attempting to salvage what can be his most precious possession—his mind."

Here we have the rare opportunity actually to observe this young woman in the process of value formation. While we cannot say with certainty exactly where the questioning process may lead, we can be sure of one thing. Without engaging in such a struggle, she will never possess principles to which she is so committed that they are unshakable.

In the previous chapter we noted Piaget's pioneering work in moral development. But while he defined the theory, it was severely limited because he proposed only two stages. After all, his research dealt entirely with children and reached only to the preteen stages. Yet neither cognitive nor moral development is complete at this point. It goes on throughout an individual's life span—at least with some individuals.

A number of different theorists have extended Piaget's work by proposing a series of moral stages covering childhood, adolescence, and adulthood. I have chosen to discuss that of Lawrence Kohlberg, not because it is necessarily better than that of others, but because it is simple and easy to understand and because—although Kohlberg was not a Christian—it provides a number of parallels to Christian moral reasoning. It is also helpful for our purposes because much of his research involved adolescents.

Kohlberg's Stages of Moral Development

Kohlberg has proposed three levels of moral development: a *preconventional level,* in which control of conduct is external both as to the standards themselves and as to the motivation for obeying them; a *conventional level,* in which control of conduct is external as to standards set by others, but motivation is largely internal, as children or youth police themselves in the same way as parents or significant others would; and a *postconventional level,* in which the control of conduct is internal, for the standards flow from an enlightened conscience, and the motivation to act is based upon an inner process of thought and judgment. At this level the moral values have validity apart from the authority of the groups or persons holding those principles.

Each level Kohlberg divided into two stages. The six stages define progressively more mature motivations that underlie moral behavior. Higher levels of moral reasoning result from increasing cognitive development and cannot go beyond it, although they can, and often do, lag behind.

Stage 1 has been labeled the punishment-obedience orientation. The motivation for behavior is to avoid punishment or to obey a superior power unquestioningly. All moral reasoning begins here, and children must pass through this stage. Punishing in some way unacceptable behavior trains the child to do right. But the reasoning of this stage may persist to some extent throughout life. A woman may obey traffic laws because she doesn't want police to ticket her. A man will refrain from stealing because he doesn't want to get caught and sent to prison. The chief motivation of some Christians for doing right is to escape hell. Old Puritan preachers used it effectively, as in Jonathan Edwards' famous sermon "Sinners in the Hands of an Angry God."

Stage 2 is the instrumental-relativist orientation. Motivation for behavior involves satisfying your own needs and sometimes those of others if they will reward you in return. It is a step up from stage 1 in that it is no longer motivated by fear, but it is still self-centered. It asks: "What's in it for *me?*" In religion it comes out as: "It pays to serve Jesus." We can go from awarding ribbons for perfect attendance to paying a faithful tithe so that when storms or plagues destroy the neighbors' crops, we are sitting in a cocoon of protection. Of course, the big payoff is heaven, the streets of gold, and eternal life.

Please note that the behaviors under the first two stages are not bad. Driving carefully, being honest, and paying tithe are good things. Also the motivations are not bad either. None of us wants a traffic ticket, a prison term, or the destruction of property. Most of us hope to be saved from eternal loss and granted everlasting life in the earth made new. But the reasoning behind the behaviors is not highly principled. It is basically self-centered. Not that care for self is inappropriate, but that higher levels of moral reasoning take one beyond merely self-concerns.

Kohlberg named the second level *conventional* because he felt that most teenagers and adults operated at this level, and that few people advanced beyond that plateau of moral reasoning. It also has two stages.

Stage 3 is the good boy–nice girl orientation. Behavior results from the desire to please others and gain their approval. An important question is: "What will they think of me?" I was once a member of a congregation that sought to raise money for a worthy cause. The church assigned each of us a personal goal. Then to motivate us to reach that goal, congregational leaders had a creative idea. They put a large chart up in front of the sanctuary with the names of each member on it. Next to the name they wrote the amount that the person had reached so far and updated it each week. The plan was quite successful. Imagine how it would feel to sit there throughout the service and look at your name with a big fat zero after it! The cause was good, but the motivation was not very principled.

A man may be polite, gracious, and pious at church but a raging tyrant at home. I may give a large donation to the building fund (preferably in public), minister to the poor, and even go to foreign fields to serve. (Once I heard someone say that his life ambition was to be a *returned* missionary.) But why am I doing such things? Is this why Jesus said: "When you give to the needy, do not let your left hand know what your right hand is doing" (Matt. 6:3, NIV)?

Stage 4 is the law-and-order orientation. Respect for law now drives behavior. People do their duty and maintain the given social order for its own sake. This area is a tough one for conservative Christians because we believe that both God's law and human laws are important and need to be obeyed. The problem comes when we do not consider law's effects on people—when law becomes more important than the situation it seeks to regulate. I was once a principal of a Christian boarding high school. Some of the faculty urged that we compile every possible infraction of school rules and then list the punishment for each violation. That way the faculty could just look at the list and automatically hand out the discipline. I resisted this approach, for it did not take into consideration motivation, previous record, background, or attitudes. Students and everyone else deserve more personal treatment.

At this stage we might promote an-eye-for-an-eye-and-a-tooth-for-a-tooth mentality, as the Pharisees of Jesus' day did. My pastor once observed that with that mentality we will all end up eyeless and toothless. Suppose that Jesus worked in a stage 4 mode. One day the religious leaders drag before Him a woman caught in adultery (John 8:2-11). "The law of Moses says that such a woman should be stoned to death," they press. "What do you say?"

Jesus replies: "Are you sure that's what it says?"

"You bet," they answer. "Here's the reference right here."

Jesus studies the scroll. "I guess you're right. That's too bad. I would really like to save her, but the law is the law. Go ahead and stone her." Of course, it didn't happen that way, because Jesus reasoned far higher than stage 4. (We will look at His way of thinking further at stage 6.) Stage 4 people wouldn't break laws even though they might be oppressive and unjust. They wouldn't have signed up as conductors on the pre-Civil War Underground Railroad to help slaves escape their masters or harmonized with Ellen White when she counseled disobedience to fugitive slave laws.

I in no way intend to belittle the concept of law. Both divine and human laws are vital for moral behavior and functioning society. Rather our discussion calls into question the practice of *legalism*—the observance of law for its own sake, regardless of how it serves God and our fellow humans. Even so, law-and-order morality is on a more mature level than the first three stages. But let's go higher.

Researchers have labeled stage 5 the social contact orientation. Seeking to maximize social utility and provide for the common good, it views moral behavior as that which is best for the majority of people. At the *postconventional level* concern turns away from one's self (first three stages) and concrete law (fourth stage) to caring about other people and what is good for them. The individual tries to keep from violating the rights or denying the needs of fellow humans. We might represent this level by the First Amendment to the United States Constitution, which guarantees freedom of speech and religion. A

Christian family holding a council to decide on standards for the home also reflects stage 5 behavior. Each member has input, and each respects the positions and feelings of all the others. And each commits to follow the agreed-upon standards because they will provide the most harmonious family life.

The Pinnacle of Principled Thinking

Stage 6 is the universal ethical principle orientation. Its motivation for behavior results from following a conscience guided by self-chosen ethical principles that appeal to logical comprehensiveness, universality, and consistency and that are based on justice and fairness for everyone, respect for the dignity of all human beings, and mutual trust. They are comprehensive because they cover every area of life, universal because they apply to all societies in every age, and consistent because they do not vary with situations.

Such principles are abstract rather than specific. An excellent example is the golden rule: "In everything, do to others what you would have them do to you, for this sums up the Law and the Prophets" (Matt. 7:12, NIV). Another is Immanuel Kant's categorical imperative: "Act only on that maxim that will enable you at the same time to will that it be a universal law." (For example, if you don't want to live in a world filled with trash, don't throw that candy wrapper on the ground.)

While stage 6 people are extremely rare—at least on a consistent basis—a consideration of their mode of thinking provides an insight into the direction that moral development will ideally take. They are not afraid of punishment or swayed by rewards like those in the first two stages. Indeed, they may take actions that they know will cost them dearly. Think of the apostles boldly defying the religious of authority of their day when it commanded them not to speak in the name of Jesus (Acts 4:18-20).

Unlike stage 3 inhabitants, they do what is right according to their inner ideals regardless of the reactions of others in their immediate environments. Stage 6 thinkers are not always admired. And while they share with stage 4 a respect for law, they know that law must serve people and not vice versa. Thus Jesus—the epitome of a stage 6 thinker—could defend the gathering of grain on the Sabbath by His hungry disciples.

In the story (Mark 2:23-28) Jesus and His disciples were walking by the grain field. Having been busy ministering all morning to others, they were now hungry. Since their world had no restaurants at every intersection, they begin to eat the only food available—the kernels of grain. Local custom allowed this as long as you ate on the spot and didn't carry any away—something like our buffets. The problem was that it was the Sabbath. The Pharisees taught that what the disciples did was harvesting grain and then, by rubbing away the chaff, threshing it. So they accused the disciples of Sabbathbreaking.

Now, if I had been Jesus, I probably would have replied, "Come on! You are really stretching it. Eating a few heads of grain is *not* harvesting or threshing." But Jesus doesn't take that angle. Rather He cites other instances of breaking rules in order to meet human need. His punch line: "The sabbath was made for humankind, and not humankind for the sabbath" (verse 27, NRSV). Thus He clearly sets out the principle that human need must trump general restrictions.

In another example, Kohlberg places at stage 6 reasoning a letter written by Martin Luther King, Jr., while a prisoner in a Birmingham, Alabama, jail. In part it read:

"One may well ask: 'How can you advocate breaking some laws and obeying others?' The answer lies in the fact that there are two types of laws: just and unjust. . . . One has not only a legal but a moral responsibility to obey just laws. Conversely, one has a moral responsibility to disobey unjust laws. . . . An unjust law is a human law that is not rooted in eternal law and natural law. Any law that uplifts human personality is just. Any law that degrades human personality is unjust."

Stage 6 thinkers do what they believe to be right regardless of the reactions of others in their immediate vicinity. The only punishment they fear is the self-condemnation of failing to be true to themselves. In the words of William Shakespeare: "To thine own self be true, and it must follow, as the night the day, thou canst not then be false to any man."

None of these stages are "bad"—children must pass through them, and we find sincere youth and adults at every step. But they do represent a progression from mere good behavior to genuine principled thinking and thus encapsulate what values development is all about.

Now, what does all this have to do with understanding the spiritual experience of adolescents? A great deal. First, we need to recognize the level of moral reasoning that any given adolescent may employ. Unless we grasp the motivations behind an action, we don't know how to appeal to the teenager. Kohlberg held that people at the lower stages cannot comprehend the reasoning of those more than one stage above them. To avoid speaking a "foreign language" when attempting to help youth, we need to be able to address them at their level.

But beyond that, parents, teachers, and other interested adults have a responsibility to facilitate the upward movement of adolescents through the moral stages. While we accept children, youth, and adults at any stage of their development, we don't leave them there. We want to stimulate growth.

Finally, we want to motivate the teenager to choose behavior in harmony with his or her highest ideals. Those interested in and responsible for the spiritual development of our young people could have no more significant task. We will suggest some ways to do this in a later chapter, but first let's look at some other theories of moral development.

CHAPTER 6

The Journey of Faith

hen Alice in *Alice in Wonderland* tried to find her way through the strange world, she asked the Cheshire Cat: "Would you tell me, please, which way I ought to go from here?"

"That depends a good deal on where you want to get to," said the Cat.

"I don't care much where—" said Alice.

"Then it doesn't matter which way you go," said the Cat.

In life, as in Wonderland, you'd better know the destination or goal, or you will never arrive there. Our goal is to help adolescents develop into spiritually mature adults who will serve both God and their fellow humans. As we have seen, maturity is a process that comes in stages.

Piaget and Kohlberg have helped us understand something about the stages of moral reasoning. We learned that moral maturity is dependent on cognitive maturity and thus—to some extent—on chronological age. Even more important, we discovered that moral maturity relates not solely to behavior but to the reasoning behind such behavior. In short, morality involves thoughtful, deliberate judgment.

But morality is not the same as spirituality. It does not necessarily involve religion at all. People who claim no religion may be highly moral. So the schemes of Piaget and Kohlberg are not speaking to religion, although, as we have seen, it is possible to apply aspects of them to the spiritual realm. So has anyone tried to translate these understandings into levels of faith? Yes. Let us look briefly at a couple examples.

James Fowler's Stages of Faith[1]

The best-known theorist here is James Fowler, who proposed six stages of faith development. The number six reminds us of Kohlberg's six stages of moral development. Indeed, we find a relationship between them, though the two theories differ somewhat. The common theme is that the stages are age-related, and Fowler suggests specific ages for each one. Both agree that one cannot reach higher stages of maturity without corresponding physical and mental development.

Thus a child may love Jesus, be obedient, and be sweet and lovable. But he or she cannot experience faith the way an older person can any more than a bright 5-year-old can learn calculus. The mental structure just isn't there.

Now, frankly, I don't like Fowler very well because I find his explanations too complicated, and his labels for his stages don't clarify the concepts as simply as Kohlberg's do. This may be a lack of cognitive structure on my part. But because of his standing in the field I will try to simplify his scheme briefly. Briefly because I don't like to explain something I don't understand that well.

First, as Fowler conceptualizes faith, its structure is unrelated to the content. So faith could belong to a Christian, a Buddhist, a Muslim, or adherent of any religion. It is not *what* you believe (although we would certainly consider that important), but *how* you arrive at that belief. Thus Fowler sees faith as a verb, not a noun. It is not a creed or a system of doctrines. Most of all, he holds that "faith is an irreducibly relational phenomenon." It always deals with how we relate to God and to our fellow humans. (See Jesus' explanation in Matthew 22:37-39.)

So let's check out the stages. We should note that moving up through them does not occur automatically. Transitions between stages are often arduous processes, according to Fowler, and some adults, despite their chronological advancement, always operate with "baby" faith. Not that simple faith is bad. But many who develop cognitively in other areas can no longer be comfortable with it, which explains why young adults often leave their childhood faith, especially when exposed to college education.

Stage 1 is labeled "intuitive-projective" (I warned you this was going to be difficult), and Fowler assigns it to children 4 to 8 years of age. During this stage parents are the source of authority in religious matters. Children really have no personal faith, but adopt what they see from the parents who represent God to them since they cannot comprehend an abstract concept such as that of a deity. Since their ability to grasp abstraction is limited, symbols are their reality. Children cannot grasp that a symbol is not real in itself but stands for some greater reality behind it.

Stage 2, called "mythic-literal," might characterize children who are 6 or 7 to 11 or 12 (notice the overlap of ages between stages). Now children are able to distinguish real from unreal and to understand the concept of the imaginary. They can perform concrete operations but continue to have little capacity for abstraction or reflection. Still not ready to construct their own faith system, they tend to yield to trusted adults for conclusions and guidance. The religious beliefs they have received from others and the rituals they are used to performing give them a sense of security.

Stage 3, "synthetic-conventional" faith, is particularly crucial for our purposes. Corresponding to Erik Erikson's "identity versus role confusion stage," it involves the period of adolescence and early adulthood when youth begin to think independently from their parents and to question the things that others have told them. Young people have a growing concern with the interpersonal. Peer friendships become very important, both that of the same and opposite sexes. Adolescents begin to internalize the ideas and expectations of others and use them to construct their own value systems. They tend to compartmentalize their behavior according to what various groups expect from them. Also they respond to some groups more than others, holding them in higher estimation and valuing their ideas more.

Adolescents are finally able to think abstractly and thus develop a value system with philosophical supports. They are making progress toward knowing what they believe and why. In this stage they need adults who are sincere, genuine, and truthful as models. Adults and other role models must press the teenagers to examine their beliefs because young people face a very real danger of adopting various values without carefully thinking through what those concepts actually mean.

At this point Fowler interjects a transition between stage 3 and 4. Adolescents begin to notice contradictions and inconsistencies in the actions and ideas of the important people in their lives. Adults whom they have admired now turn out to have feet of clay. They don't always live up to what they preach. Also teenagers discover that beliefs they had thought to be inviolable can change or be wrong. Some of the things they have been taught no longer agree with facts in the wider world. Often young people find themselves forced to do critical reflection on their childhood beliefs. It is a momentous time. Which way will they go? Will their faith survive?

Stage 4 Fowler called "individuative-reflective." It lasts from 17 or 18 years of age into the early 20s. The transaction to this stage can be a protracted process. But if successful, it results in a faith that is personal, consistent, and logical. Here young people not only have learned how to evaluate the various influences on their lives, but take responsibility for their own commitments.

Stage 5 is labeled "conjunctive" faith, and rarely appears before age 30. It evolves from deepening life experience and is, therefore, inaccessible to those who have not lived a while. People have faced suffering, loss, and injustice, and have had to meet and deal with the problem of evil. They have had time to sort out life's inconsistencies. By now the values they have developed have been verified not only by others but by their own inner method of relating to the transcendent. Such individuals are open to the inadequacy of commitment and the possibility of an uncertain future. At this stage it becomes clear to them that their knowledge of reality is only partial, and that they must be willing to shift their thinking as they acquire an increasing understanding of the world.

Stage 6 finally reaches the epitome. Fowler called it "universalizing" faith and declared that it is exceedingly rare. As examples, he listed Martin Luther King, Jr., Mother Teresa, and Dag Hammarskjöld. At this stage one develops an overwhelming passion and commitment to love and to justice. A desire to serve fellow humans and to make the world a better place replaces the focus on meeting personal needs.

Fowler asks us to notice two points about faith development. First, while Christian faith is concerned with content, faith development studies how faith grows, the changes that happen in a person, and how faith affects the life. Second, we should not evaluate individuals by their current stage. No stage is "bad." All who achieve a mature faith will pass through all of these stages—at least as far as they progress. Rather, it is the task of those involved in youth ministry to nurture the faith of children and adolescents, helping them to reach the highest stage of which they are capable.

To accomplish this, Fowler suggests some strategies for ministering to the faith concerns of adolescents. Adults should:

1. Share their own faith walk with young people.
2. Identify the roles of the youth and help them to discover how they feel about them.
3. Pose "Why?" questions about the various values under consideration.
4. Encourage youth to look at perspectives that differ from their own.
5. Explore the meaning of God and Jesus as a friend.
6. Examine what it means to be a Christian and a person of faith.
7. Foster reflective critiques of personal and social values.

Bailey Gillespie's Faith Situations[2]

Gillespie, a professor of theology at La Sierra University, has also attempted to construct a model that would explain how faith develops. He prefers not to use the word "stages" because he is not proposing a formal model, but rather presents seven "situations" identified through observation. However, the situations resemble stages, especially those proposed by James Fowler. The labels are more intuitive and thus easier to understand. But the same progression from the simple to the complex emerges. Since Gillespie has assigned age groups to each situation, they serve the same function as stages. Regardless of chronological age, however, the key is the developing of cognitive abilities. The youth must reach certain levels of mental ability in order to have mature faith—especially the ability to think abstractly. We can easily see this relationship in the label and ages assigned to each situation.

Situation 1: "borrowed faith"—early childhood. Children learn to trust their parents and adopt their faith.

Situation 2: "reflected faith"—middle childhood. Parents shape not only the child's understanding of faith, but also that of others from outside the home. Young people learn to become involved in the church and find in it a community of faith. This is also the time they identify with great heroes of the faith as they absorb the Bible stories.

Situation 3: "personalized faith"—early adolescence. The situation of greatest interest to our study, it is the period in which youth will begin to make their faith personal. It involves reflection, critical evaluation, and perhaps rejection of some aspects of childhood faith. Building upon the new ability to abstract, investigate, and place one's self in the viewpoints of others, independent thinking develops, something that emotionally involved adults may regard as rebellion.

Situation 4: "interior faith" or "established faith"—later youth. After the sorting and questioning time comes a period of commitment. Young people have established their faith and no longer spend time probing it. Religious questions may take a back seat to other concerns.

Situation 5: "reordered faith"—young adults. Here once again theological reflection becomes important, and the personal commitment they developed earlier may undergo reinterpretation as they discover more of the world.

Situation 6: "reflective faith"—middle adults. It is the time people decide what they want their life to accomplish. They reduce life to the basics and view it in very broad perspectives. They do not, however, focus on issues of ultimate concern.

Situation 7: "resolute faith"—older adults. As they review life's choices, they commit to a faith that will sustain and comfort them through the retirement years and help them face their own mortality.

Two comments seem appropriate here. First, individuals mature physically, mentally, and spiritually at different rates. Therefore, we cannot be rigid in applying the age groups to the particular situations. Some may never get beyond the early descriptions.

Second, we must have realistic expectations. Small children cannot have personalized faith, and we should not be disappointed that they don't. Teenagers will not have the reordered faith or the reflective faith of thinking adults who have had to meet life's challenges and test their own spiritual experience. Youth workers must be willing to accept adolescents at their current stage or situation and nurture them as they face the challenges of developing an ever-increasing faith.

Marcia's Search for a Sense of Identity[3]

Building on the work of other theorists, James Marcia has presented faith development as a process of identity achievement. As a person proceeds from childhood to adulthood, one of the chief tasks is to form a sense of self-identity. "Who am I?" is the existential question. Each person needs to discover his or her own religious values, interpersonal relationships, vocational goals, and potential as a marriage partner, as well as to develop a philosophy of life. It requires deep searching to put it all together in an authentic manner. Marcia has proposed four identity statuses that describe the different ways youth go about this crucial task.

He builds his four statuses on the concepts of *crisis* and *commitment*. *Crisis* here refers to a challenge to the existing way of constructing reality (beliefs about the world) that results in cognitive dissonance and motivates the person to explore alternative and competing roles and ideologies as a means of reducing that dissonance. *Commitment* refers to the act of selecting from competing alternatives a way of organizing and understanding reality and then locking into that choice in a way not easily reversed or abandoned. With that background in mind we will look at the four statuses.

In *identity diffusion* adolescents lack personal commitment and have not experienced anything that compels them to search for a cause to which they can commit. We might say that not only have they not found—they are not even yet looking. In *identity foreclosure* adolescents commit themselves to a certain set of beliefs, often as a result of parental influences, and are not yet open to examining or questioning their present convictions. They have either never faced the challenge of a crisis or have refused to engage in any process that would upset their present comfortable reality. This use of "commitment," according to Clifford T. Morgan, describes the tendency of many youth to freeze or crystallize their attitudes so that they do not change much afterward. It is their coping strategy for reducing cognitive dissonance.[4] In effect they say: "My mind is made up—don't confuse me with the facts." While they may seem to have strong values, the appearance is deceptive because those values really belong to someone else. Because they have not internalized them, such values are unlikely to withstand a real test in the unprotected world.

In *moratorium* adolescents are presently in a state of crisis and are attempting to resolve it through carefully examining life's various options. But while they have not yet committed, they have begun on the journey. This is the healthy way to find a personal faith. Finally, in *identity achievement,* adolescents have gone through the crisis, faced the challenges, carefully explored the options, and have deliberately chosen their answers on the basis of the evidence. Their commitment is stable because they have personally internalized it.

The large majority of teens tend to be in the status of either diffusion or foreclosure. In order to enhance spiritual development and faith maturity, then, Christian leaders need to encourage such youth to move out from diffusion or foreclosure through moratorium to a responsible identity achievement.

It means that we must not only permit but encourage teenagers to question our value statements, something that is not easy to do. Naturally drawn to the conforming, obedient youth who affirms our position, we feel uncomfortable in the presence of the critical one who "makes waves." If we are honest, we will admit that we have usually reinforced agreement rather than questioning. But we *must* press adolescents to raise the questions, to identify the important issues, and to think through to the solutions, or they will reach adulthood with a set of "values" that can easily collapse and disappear in a crisis simply because they have never personally committed themselves to them.

Does this mean that our heritage from the past is worthless? Must youth begin from scratch without benefit of the winnowed wisdom of the ages? Certainly not! Rollo May sets the situation in perspective by showing that the battle is over not individual freedom versus tradition (here meaning anything handed down to us), but how tradition is to be used. The authoritarian asks, "What does the tradition require of me?" The free person inquires, "What does the tradition have to teach me about human life in my particular time and with my special problems and challenges?"[5]

By understanding the stages and the situations of faith development and the young person's search for identity, we are better able to help adolescents progress toward a mature faith. But what is a mature faith? We'll take that up next.

---

[1] Summary drawn from James W. Fowler, *Stages of Faith: The Psychology of Human Development and the Quest for Meaning* (San Francisco: Harper & Row, 1981).

[2] See V. Bailey Gillespie, *The Experience of Faith* (Birmingham, Ala.: Religious Education Press, 1988), for a full development of these situations.

[3] For a summary and discussion of Marcia's theory, see John Van Wicklin, Ronald Burwell, and Richard Butman, "Squandered Years: Identity Foreclosed Students and the Liberal Education They Avoid," in D. John Lee and Gloria Goris Stronks, eds., *Assessment in Christian Higher Education: Rhetoric and Reality* (Lanham, Md.: University Press of America, Inc., 1994), pp. 75-103. For a stage theory of identity development, see Erik Erikson, *Identity: Youth and Crisis* (New York: Norton, 1968).

[4] See Clifford T. Morgan, *A Brief Introduction to Psychology*, second ed. (New York: McGraw-Hill Book Co., 1977), p. 392.

[5] See Rollo May, *Man's Search for Himself* (New York: W. W. Norton, 1953).

CHAPTER 7

A Picture of Mature Faith

It was after hours, but I was still working in my office when the knock came at the door. I opened it to greet a solitary student holding a ready-for-action King James Version Bible. "May I ask you a question?" he inquired. When I nodded my approval, he began to read from 2 Chronicles 16:9: "The eyes of the Lord run to and fro throughout the whole earth, to shew himself strong in the behalf of them whose heart is perfect toward him."

Pausing, he looked up. "My question is: What does it mean to be perfect?"

What indeed! Christians have struggled with this question for centuries. Does it indicate a state of absolute sinlessness? Does it connote a mystical experience in which we apprehend the presence of the divine in extrasensory ways? Does it point to flawless theology or an exhaustive grasp of the "real truth"? Is it a Mother Teresa-like life of selfless service? Is it stricter adherence to a certain code of behavior than that achieved by most mortals—a virtuoso religiosity?

We will not settle this complex question in this brief chapter. Yet in the light of our search for mature faith certain aspects are worth considering. The New International Version rendering of the passage that the student brought to my attention reads "fully committed," suggesting a direction of the will and heart. In Ephesians 4:13 Paul called upon Christians to come "unto a perfect man, unto the measure of the stature of the fulness of Christ." The marginal reading is "full-grown," and the NIV renders the phrase "become mature."

The implication is that perfection is an experience of growth (stages?) within a wholehearted commitment. The individual's faith steadily matures toward the standard set by Jesus Himself. Ellen White wrote: "At every stage [note the use of her term] of development our life may be perfect; yet if God's purpose for us is fulfilled, there will be continual advancement."[1]

We seek to help adolescents to grow toward that mature faith. In our exploration of the stages of faith we have seen that faith is dependent on cognitive development, that mature faith is more than just right behavior but involves motivation, and that its focus moves from self-interest to concern for others. Still, we are trying to get a better picture of what the goal would look like if we reached it. I'd like us to consider two proposals—one based on content and one on process.

Faith Maturity—Valuegenesis[2]

First I wish to examine one picture of "faith maturity," paying special attention to the implications of the widely heralded Valuegenesis study. Valuegenesis utilized a pioneering way of assessing faith maturity, developed from 1988 to 1990 by Search Institute for a nationwide study of adults and youth in six national Protestant denominations.

In this conceptual scheme faith maturity is not simply a set of right beliefs, although beliefs do figure in. Rather, it is conceived more as a way of life, as a set of priorities, dispositions, and behaviors that indicate that one's faith is deep, vibrant, and life-changing. A person of mature faith integrates into his or her life eight core dimensions of faith. Such a person:

1. Trusts in God's saving grace and believes firmly in the humanity and divinity of Jesus.
2. Experiences a sense of personal well-being, security, and peace.
3. Integrates faith and life, seeing work, family, social relationships, and political choices as part of one's religious life.

4. Seeks spiritual growth through study, reflection, prayer, and discussion with others.
5. Seeks to be part of a community of believers in which people give witness to their faith and support and nourish one another.
6. Holds life-affirming values, including commitment to racial and gender equality.
7. Advocates social and global change to bring about greater social justice.
8. Serves humanity, consistently and passionately, through acts of love and justice.

The developers of the study constructed within each of the eight core dimensions representative statements of mature faith. The mature faith scale used a total of 38, and they comprise the first 38 items in the Valuegenesis questionnaire. The researchers averaged the responses to them, creating for each person a mature faith score that could range from 1 to 7. A score between 1.00 and 2.99 indicates low faith maturity, between 3.00 and 4.99 moderate faith maturity, and 5.00 or above high faith maturity.

The average faith maturity score for all 10,641 Adventist youth attending Adventist schools was 4.44, which is in the moderate range. Faith maturity tended to drop slightly after the sixth grade but to remain relatively stable between grades 7 to 12. About 22 percent of the sample were in the high faith maturity category, with the highest proportion in grade 6 (29 percent) and the lowest in grades 10 and 11 (20 percent). The drop in scores shows that what is being measured here is different from the faith development described in stage theories.

Types of Faith

Two themes run through the mature faith index: the *vertical* theme of having a deep, personal relationship with a loving God, and the *horizontal* theme of translating this personal affirmation into acts of love, mercy, and justice toward others. If we select certain items from the 38 in the full index, it is possible to construct two subscales—one for vertical faith and the other for horizontal faith. On these seven-point subscales Adventist youth averaged 4.8 (or moderate) for vertical faith. Horizontal faith was somewhat lower at 4.0. Our young people seemed more likely to relate to God than to their fellow humans.

The scores for these two subscales were split at the median (middle score) to determine whether a given individual could be classified as high (more than 4.05) on horizontal faith or high (more than 5.26) on vertical faith. Each person could then be classified into one of four faith types as follows:

undeveloped faith	low on both vertical and horizontal faith
vertical faith	high on vertical but low on horizontal faith
horizontal faith	high on horizontal but low on vertical faith
integrated faith	high on both vertical and horizontal faith

The findings reveal that 43 percent of all Adventist youth had an undeveloped faith, in which both the vertical and the horizontal dimensions are relatively low, 8 percent were classified as having vertical faith, 24 percent possessed horizontal faith, and 25 percent had reached an integrated faith in which they were high on both dimensions. Any change across age groups, though slight, seemed to be of a negative nature. The percentage with undeveloped faith was at a low in grade 6 (38 percent), rose to a high in grades 8 and 9 (45 percent), and dropped slightly by grade 12 (42 percent). The percentage with integrated faith ranged from 35 percent in grade 6 to 22 percent in grade 11, with seniors coming back up to 26 percent.

The proportion of Adventist youth with undeveloped faith (43 percent) was lower than that of any of the five mainline Protestant denominations in the national study conducted by Search Institute, which ranged from 56 percent to 68 percent, though slightly higher than Southern Baptist youth at 40 percent. Conversely, the 25 percent with integrated faith was higher than that of any of the mainline churches (ranging from 6 to 13 percent), but lower than that of the Southern Baptists, which had 30 percent in that group. The Southern Baptist Convention has rated comparatively well by, in part, placing high emphasis on developing and maintaining effective religious education programs delivered through congregations. None of these six denominations has produced an alternative school system comparable to that found among Adventists. The results may suggest a need to restudy our congregational religious education program (Sabbath schools).

Compared to mainline Protestantism, the Adventist Church seems to be doing quite well in faith development. Nevertheless, the fact that more than four out of 10 of our adolescents are marked by an undeveloped faith is a cause for concern, in part because persons with such undeveloped faith are particularly prone to slip into life-long church inactivity.

Predictors of Mature Faith

Examining the kinds of attitudes and behaviors that accompany mature faith—the lifestyle package, if you will—will increase our understanding of the nature of faith and its development. While the correlation of two variables does not prove that one causes the other, it does generate some possible directions that may prove fruitful in further study. Therefore, using the statistical technique of multiple regression analysis, the researchers correlated a number of other variables with the mature faith scale in an effort to determine what other practices might best "predict" maturity of faith.

Taking all of these relationships together, the most important predictor of mature faith was a scale labeled "value of service." It consisted of four items that the youth rated as to their importance: "to spend time helping people," "to help people who are poor or hungry," "to show love to other people," and "to help promote social equality." Apparently, when we are able to help young people accept and live by those values, we foster the development of faith maturity.

The second most important predictor of mature faith was a scale titled "personal piety." Here youth reported the frequency in which they engaged in five devotional practices: prayer, watching or listening to religious programs, reading the Bible, reading Ellen White, and reading religious literature. While the "value of service" attitudes encourage the development of horizontal faith, the "personal piety" practices enhance vertical faith, and the two together lead to faith maturity.

Other important predictors were a grace orientation to salvation, having a purpose in life, and the perception of a positive thinking climate in the local congregation. We will return to them later.

A "Process" Measure

The validity of the foregoing depends, of course, on whether one accepts the eight core dimensions as an accurate concept of mature faith and, second, whether one assumes that the questions in the scale measure the concept accurately. While I happen to believe that the conceptual scheme has merit and that the measurements are reasonably accurate, you are probably aware that the mature faith scale has triggered some criticism.

Some have contended that phrases such as "commitment to racial and gender equality" and "advocates social change to bring about greater social justice" are not elements of mature faith at all but represent a secular social activism or a liberal "social gospel." Other dimensions carry specific theological content (with which Adventists would probably agree) that might not apply to members of all faith communities. So without in any way discounting what I have presented thus far, let us examine the subject from another perspective. We might profit from exploring briefly a relatively "content-free" process model. In other words: What would faith maturity look like from a psychological frame of reference?

As early as 1937 Harvard psychologist Gordon Allport argued that a mature personality has three general attributes: (1) a variety of psychogenic interests that concern themselves with ideals and values beyond the range of immediate biological impulses or drives; (2) the ability to objectify oneself, to be reflective and insightful about one's own life, including a developed sense of humor; and (3) some unifying philosophy of life.[3]

Allport explained that such attributes had not been selected arbitrarily but had been chosen because they represent the three primary avenues of development open to any human being in the course of his or her growth: the avenue of widening interests (the expanding self), the avenue of detachment and insight (self-objectification), and the avenue of integration (self-unification). He doubted that any scientifically supported criteria of maturity would differ substantially from these three.[4]

By 1950 Allport was ready to apply these characteristics to the religious experience. The criteria of religious maturity, he believed, should be drawn from a defensible theory of the nature of human personality. Thus he proposed six attributes that distinguished the mature religious outlook from the immature variety.[5] I will list each one with a brief explanation. Mature faith is:

1. *Well-differentiated.* Religiously mature persons are conscious of the richness and complexity of their religion. They are aware that each religious issue has many facets, and therefore they do not oversimplify reality. They can recognize the strengths and the weaknesses, the good points and the shortcomings, of their religious beliefs and practices. Nor do they see everything in black and white, but discern the fine shades of gray in between. As a result, they are involved in a continuous examination and reorganization of their religious beliefs. Though they are critical (in the best sense of the word) of their faith, they are also articulate about it.

2. *Dynamic in character in spite of its derivative nature.* The beginnings of religious faith are rooted in the drives and desires of the body. That is, the child (of any age) turns to religion to conquer fears, gain rewards, and escape punishments. While this is normal, religiously immature people continue to view religion instrumentally—they use it for what they can get out of it. By contrast, mature religion is less of a servant and more of a master in the economy of life. Free from being goaded and steered exclusively by impulse, fear, or wish, it tends rather to control and to direct the motives toward goals that are no longer determined by mere self-interest. It asks not, "What can my religion do for me?" but "What can I do for my religion, my God, and the world?"

3. *Productive of a consistent morality.* While those who are religiously immature may sporadically alter their conduct, they tend to wall off certain areas of morality from the influence of their religion. By contrast, mature religionists let their faith inform and shape every area of

their moral action. Their behavior toward their fellow humans is steadily consistent with their faith.

4. *Comprehensive.* The religiously mature person's faith must address all the crucial questions of life and provide workable answers. Such religion does not become absorbed with narrow interests or ride only theological hobbyhorses. It has a widened interest in both this world and the next. The demand for comprehensiveness also makes for tolerance. One knows that one's life alone does not contain all possible values or all facets of meaning. Other people too have their stake in truth, because it is just too broad for any one mind to encompass. The religion of maturity makes the affirmation "God is," but only the religion of immaturity will insist that "God is precisely what I say He is."

5. *Integral.* Closely allied to the demand for comprehensiveness is the insistence of mature persons that religion compose a homogeneous pattern. Not only must its coverage be great, but its design must be harmonious. It must infuse and be able to explain all of life. The religiously mature person will not compartmentalize or isolate religion from other aspects of the world. The most difficult of all facts to integrate into a total worldview is the problem of evil. Yet this issue also—perhaps especially—must be faced and fought through, or otherwise the religion cannot become mature.

6. *Fundamentally heuristic.* The adjective "heuristic" means aiding or guiding in discovery. Thus an heuristic belief is one that people hold tentatively until they can confirm it or until it helps them discover a more valid belief. Those who are religiously mature do not pompously imagine that they have the last word—that they alone are in possession of all truth. They know that advancing time and new knowledge may cause them to modify their present beliefs. Truth may be absolute, but our possession of it is always partial and—from the perspective of maturity—progressive. Yet mature individuals are committed to their religion, for they understand it to be the most satisfying explanation of reality according to their present light. The mature mind can act wholeheartedly even without absolute certainty. It can be sure without being cocksure. It has both the firmness to live

by present truth and the humility to bow to new illumination.

Each of the models of faith development contributes to a multifaceted picture of what mature faith might look like. As we interact with various adolescents, we can see where their thinking and behavior fits into this overall scheme. More important, understanding the models provides us with practical suggestions and directions for helping such youth grow toward the higher stages. We must know what the goal is if we hope to reach it. But can we find some overarching religious framework into which we can fit all this information? We will look at that next.

---

[1] Ellen G. White, *Christ's Object Lessons* (Washington, D.C.: Review and Herald Pub. Assn., 1900), p. 65.

[2] The next several sections are from Roger L. Dudley with V. Bailey Gillespie, *Valuegenesis: Faith in the Balance* (Riverside, Calif.: La Sierra University Press, 1992), pp. 57-79.

[3] Gordon W. Allport, *Personality: A Psychological Interpretation* (New York: Henry Holt and Co., 1937), pp. 213-231.

[4] Gordon W. Allport, *The Individual and His Religion* (New York: Macmillan, 1950), p. 53.

[5] *Ibid.*, p. 57.

The Gospel Key

As I grow older, I am beginning to feel that I'm not important to the church. Our Sabbath school is a joke, because it's the department that gets leftovers for teachers. When I'm home from school, I just skip Sabbath school, because it eliminates the frustrations I feel when I try to lead the teacher into topics that really matter, but to no avail. Then instead of receiving a normal bulletin when I walk into church, I'm handed one with no cover on it from the bottom of the pile. The next people [adults] who come in get normal ones. Sometimes I don't get one at all. The greeter says, 'If no more people come in, I'll come give you one.' I know this sounds very silly, and it is, but it is those little things that add up and make people feel just a little less important. Maybe it is a lot of 'little' reasons that make people want to leave the church. I just wish my home church would treat me like an adult. Is that too much to ask?"

The preceding comment comes from a teenage girl enrolled in our 10-year youth study of more than 1,500 teenagers spread across the entire North American Division. Through the years we have received hundreds of comments from these youth sharing how they see their congregations. Some of them are very positive. But many complain that the church doesn't seem to relate to them. Let's look at a few more responses.

"I see discontent and boredom among those in our age group, and

I wish so badly the other youth and I could find enthusiasm. But it's very difficult to want to be involved when our ideas and opinions are considered to be too radical and not important. Everyone tells us we are the church of tomorrow, but I and millions of others are trying to tell you and anyone else who will listen that there will be no church of tomorrow if we are not recognized, accepted as we are, and allowed to put our youthful energy and new ideas into effect. Time moves forward, not backward—just like science and technology."

"I have personal problems that to others may seem like nothing but to me are really important. I feel alone. I need more than just a spiritual feeling. I need a mortal feeling. I need a person to love, feel, touch, care, and talk to. I need a special friend I can trust and make me feel wanted."

"It's so true that many times Adventist standards don't make sense to youth. This comes as a result of emphasizing standards and not a love relationship with Jesus. Also, it comes as a result of double standards in older members. I, along with many other young people, want to see Christians that live their lives as Christians, not just going through motions and playing church once a week. We're unimpressed and turned off by Adventists that say they belong to the church and yet don't care for others, hoard money for their own gain, etc. These are the kinds of living examples that send messages that God is good, but let's get on with life. 'I don't have time in my busy schedule for you. Sorry.' The youth around me are crying out for living, breathing Christianity. Our lives are attacked in so many ways, ways that never really affected the young lives of those before us. Though drugs, sex, general immorality, and family problems are not entirely new, the amount is. As these issues are addressed again and again at Bible conferences, youth leadership workshops, and Pathfinder worships, I'm frustrated. The root cause isn't being touched upon nearly as often as the symptoms. Youth are hurting because of lack of love and acceptance, lack of self-worth, but most of all because they don't know Jesus. Let's speak to this issue first; then with this in mind help with things like drugs (for example). We will probably have more success."

The Complex Religion of Teens

"I think the key factors in keeping the youth in the church are personal relationships with Christ and positive involvement in church activities. They need encouragement in the positive aspects of their involvements. Young people need to see that religion makes a difference in one's life. We need to see that being an Adventist affects all aspects of life."

"I am sick of the rules they pile on us. People that wouldn't normally break rules do, because there are so many. After that it becomes easier to break more."

"I support the Adventist Church completely, but I also have some problems with it. I think that the reason the church loses so many youth is that the youth see the church as not inviting, and the reason for this is that they don't realize that they need to have a relationship with Christ. They see the rules as legalistic and something they have to do instead of realizing that they should keep the commandments because of their relationship with Christ, not just to be an Adventist member."

"Our church has so many unnecessary rules. The leaders become so concerned about petty little things. Our religion has become too legalistic! We should be concerned about teaching others to know Christ, but first we need to learn to keep the youth in the church before we try to convince others. You can't try to teach others that it's the true way if you can't teach your own people. I don't know how to do this, and I doubt anything will be done about it, but if something doesn't happen soon, there won't be any youth left in the church to worry about."

"I feel very confused and frustrated with the Adventist Church and my religion right now. I've seen, heard, and understood all the whys of our church doctrines all my life. I even agree with 99.9 percent of it. But what is bothering me now is the lack of love, unity, and honest people trying to live like Jesus seven days a week instead of just Sabbath. Of what meaning are our doctrines if we don't show God's love unconditionally to everyone?"

"The Adventist Church carries its legalistic approach to Christianity a bit too far. All these rules, regulations, and other stuff are good, and yes, they are helpful in life. Being an Adventist all of my life, I've grown up accepting all these things. But for that person who is looking for a church home, Seventh-day Adventism can be a very scary ordeal. The first thing he/she learns about our church is not the love of God and how special it is to have a close relationship with Him. No. Instead he/she hears, 'Well, we Adventists have 832 rules. We don't eat all sorts of stuff, we don't smoke, we don't drink, we don't wear jewelry. Oh, I see you're wearing a ring. Well, you are definitely going to have to take it off when you join our church or else you'll go straight to hell. Have a happy Sabbath.' Naturally you know that I'm exaggerating, but it is true that we emphasize our legalism and frown upon anyone who breaks one of the commandments. It's no wonder that so many people are scared away, not only those who are considering membership but also those already in the church."

I could go on for pages, but that's enough to illustrate my point. In fairness I must repeat that I have heard from many youth who have found warm, accepting congregations and who love their churches. But the sentiments expressed above in one way or another represent hundreds of teenagers, certainly the majority of this representative sample.

So what is the major theme these adolescents are trying to tell us? They are hungry for relationships and are not finding them in the church. Very few have ever complained about the doctrines of the church. In fact, many affirm them, as the sample responses show. But they want something more than cold teachings or rules of behavior. They long for people in the church, especially adult leaders, to care about them. And most of all they seek a relationship with Jesus.

Through the years I've had personal contacts with hundreds of adolescents. Young people raised in the Adventist Church have a very difficult time internalizing salvation by grace alone. They may believe it intellectually, but their background in behavioral requirements constantly interferes with the joy of assurance in Jesus. So how can we help them achieve this mature faith we so much want them to realize?

The Complex Religion of Teens

The Framework of Relationships

Both the Valuegenesis model and the Allport process model that we have considered suggest several things that adult mentors, such as parents, teachers, and congregational leaders, can do to aid young people advance toward maturity of faith. One key direction is to approach the subject in the framework of relationships.

As I have noted, many youth who grow up in Adventist homes and attend Adventist schools arrive at the threshold of adulthood with a concept of religion that is largely behavioral. Religion consists of living up to all the standards and regulations of the church and avoiding whatever the church has branded as "sins." A woman in her 30s, who had attended an Adventist academy and two of our colleges but is not now a practicing Adventist, wrote me of her struggles with religion. "Why would God require so much of us when it is impossible for us to do it?" she wondered. "Why must religion make one feel guilty all the time?"

I would like to suggest that we need to perceive and teach religion as a set of relationships rather than as a list of commands and prohibitions. This suggestion is not addressed only, or even primarily, to those who teach courses in Bible or religion. In a Christian school teachers cannot avoid modeling a concept of religion—whatever their particular discipline. Neither can parents, pastors, or congregational leaders. It oozes out of us.

First and central to all else is a relationship with God as a loving Father and Friend. Jesus went to the very core of religion when He stated: "Love the Lord your God with all your heart and with all your soul and with all your mind. This is the first and greatest commandment" (Matt. 22:37, 38, NIV). It is interesting that the lawyer asked Jesus about the greatest *commandment*. The man phrased his question in behavioral terms. It's as if he said: "What shall I *do*?" But Jesus answered in *relational* terms—"*Love!*"

Sin, then, is not the violation of a list of required behaviors. Rather it is the breaking of this relationship—being out of harmony with God and not loving Him. The correct translation of 1 John 3:4 is "Sin is lawlessness" (NIV)—being out of alignment with the fundamental reality of the cosmos. Sin began in the universe when Lucifer tried to replace God (Isa. 14:14), and gained a foothold on earth when Eve decided she could be as wise as God—thus making Him dispensable (Gen. 3:5). Thus sin is wanting to be God ourselves. Faith is the restoration of the God–human relationship. Therefore, "everything that does not come from faith is sin" (Rom. 14:23, NIV), and "this is the victory that has overcome the world, even our faith" (1 John 5:4, NIV).

Following from this primary relationship, religion then works in our own interior relationships, eliminating anxiety and stress and bringing harmony and peace of mind. Jesus spoke of this when He said: "Peace I leave with you; my peace I give you. . . . Do not let your hearts be troubled and do not be afraid" (John 14:27, NIV). Through a relationship with God Christians can have security.

Out of this twofold relationship with God and with ourselves comes a new relationship with our fellow humans. The second greatest commandment is to "love your neighbor as yourself" (Matt. 22:39, NIV). Compassion and concern for people will characterize true Christianity. Throughout the Bible, from the cries of the Old Testament prophets for justice, through the ethical teachings of Jesus, to the detailed instruction in the latter part of the Pauline Epistles, the theme of caring for others is pervasive. When Christ discussed the great judgment day, "He represented its decision as turning upon one point. When the nations are gathered before Him, there will be but two classes, and their eternal destiny will be determined by what they have done or have neglected to do for him in the person of the poor and the suffering."[1]

On all three relationship dimensions the most effective teaching comes out of the life of the Christian. When rather than prescribing and proscribing behaviors, we model what it means to live in relationships, we best help the youth to build solid components into their personal value systems and thus grow toward faith maturity.

Educators divide values into two classes: *group-specific values* are widely shared within one group or society but have little meaning to those not in that group. A conservative church such as ours will have many—for example, proper activities for Sabbath, dietary regulations, use of jewelry, standards of recreation, giving patterns, etc. On the other hand, *abstract-universal* values describe those that would be affirmed (but not necessarily practiced) by nearly all thoughtful people. They include concepts such as equality, justice, absence of prejudice, self-respect, respect for others, responsible behavior, tolerance for varying views, honesty, compassion, etc.[2]

If we are to produce adults who determine their behavior by a set of carefully considered principles and whose religion promotes a deeper relationship between God and humanity and between people and people, I would like to suggest that we must give priority to the abstract-universal values in our efforts at moral education.

That is not to say that group-specific values are not important. Indeed, they are the qualities that give uniqueness to any community. Wash them away, and the group might as well blend into the larger society. They are its raison d'être as a separate entity.

But if we concentrate on specifics first in our transmission of values, we may well produce youth who have codes of behavior but no integrated system of principles; who are legalistic but not loving; and who have some worthwhile rules but no overarching framework in which to situate them. We need to place the primary emphasis on the larger picture of relationships and then fit the specific values into this total life pattern. Thus we must begin with the general and move to the particular.

In other words, it is foolish and futile to attempt to instill specific values in a person without regard for that individual's experience as a thinking, choosing, loving being. When one lives in relationship with God, self, and fellow humans, we can be confident that he or she will select the specific behaviors that will enhance those relationships. If the choices are somewhat different than I would have made, who am I to declare them invalid? I would rather see a principled person who disagrees with me than a mindless conformist any day.

Since relationships are so dependent on quality time together, we will need to give new emphasis to the practices that make for a rich devotional life. The Valuegenesis study and others have shown that many of our youth do not pray and read the Bible on a consistent basis. We will have to teach them how to pray conversationally rather than formally and how to use the Bible in a manner that provides spiritual nourishment. Our past experience has shown that youth revival has always been accompanied by groups who study, sing, pray, and share together. The church will need to foster more of this today. New worship materials, new opportunities, and new training in peer leadership will all provide the ferment to make this happen.

Clarify the Gospel

We have seen that though our youth have heard the *words* of the gospel of righteousness by faith, the Adventist emphasis on behavioral standards has led the majority to believe that they must somehow do something to merit salvation. It is very difficult for an Adventist adolescent to accept emotionally the fact that his or her salvation rests entirely on the merits of Jesus Christ and that he or she cannot contribute to it one whit.

In view of this tendency I think we will have to bend over backward in our homes, our congregations, and our schools to get across a grace perspective to salvation, for, as noted in the previous chapter, such an orientation is an important predictor of a mature faith. To be honest, we are a little nervous about going all out for righteousness by faith alone for fear we will push our youth into an antinomianism that will undermine obedience. But the evidence indicates that for the vast majority of adolescents disobedience results not from a grace orientation to the Gospel but from a law orientation. Young people find that they cannot measure up to the demands of the law, become discouraged, and quit trying because the task is hopeless. Since they are going to be lost anyway, they might as well enjoy whatever they can in this world.

Through precept and example, we must do everything possible to clarify grace and to break the hold of legalism. We must communicate a gospel of hope. Without such effort we will never retain our youth. They will not continue to struggle in a contest that they cannot possibly win.

The Complex Religion of Teens

The Valuegenesis project has shown us that we most effectively transmit a grace orientation to our youth not by talk, but by parents who have entered into this experience; by providing a climate of warmth and acceptance in our local congregations; and by the presence of caring teachers in our school systems. We best learn and accept grace through warm, supportive, interpersonal relationships with grace-filled people. A major task before us is to instruct our parents, teachers, and congregational leaders in how to be that kind of people.

Note that faith maturity is not a static concept—a condition attained once and for all. Rather, it is dynamic. Mature and immature are not discrete categories. Rather, maturity is a continuum on which all of us are located—some in advance of others, but none at the terminus beyond which lies no room for growth. A lifetime is none too long to travel that journey. It is this vision that we may share with our youth and these attitudes with which we may equip them if we wish them to become principled adults whose lives are lived in relationship with God, who experience inner serenity, and who bless their fellow humans because they are committed to love and justice.

---

[1] Ellen G. White, *The Desire of Ages* (Mountain View, Calif.: Pacific Press Pub. Assn., 1898), p. 637.

[2] See Margaret Edwards Arcus, "Value Reasoning: An Approach to Values Education," *Family Relations* 29 (April 1980): 163-171.

A Brand-new Life

Let's look at the religious experience of one teenager. "While bowed at the altar with others who were seeking the Lord, all the language of my heart was: 'Help, Jesus; save me, or I perish! I will never cease to entreat till my prayer is heard and my sins are forgiven.' I felt my needy, helpless condition as never before.

"As I knelt and prayed, suddenly my burden left me, and my heart was light. At first a feeling of alarm came over me, and I tried to resume my load of distress. It seemed to me that I had no right to feel joyous and happy. But Jesus seemed very near to me; I felt able to come to Him with all my griefs, misfortunes, and trials, even as the needy ones came to Him for relief when He was upon earth. There was a surety in my heart that He understood my peculiar trials, and sympathized with me. I can never forget this precious assurance of the pitying tenderness of Jesus toward one so unworthy of His notice. I learned more of the divine character of Christ in that short period, when bowed among the praying ones, than ever before.

"One of the mothers in Israel came to me and said, 'Dear child, have you found Jesus?' I was about to answer, 'Yes,' when she exclaimed, 'Indeed you have; His peace is with you, I see it in your face!'

"Again and again I said to myself: 'Can this be religion? Am I not mistaken?' It seemed too much for me to claim, too exalted a privilege. Though too timid to confess it openly, I felt that the Savior had blessed me and pardoned my sins. . . .

The Complex Religion of Teens

"Now the sun shone bright and clear, and flooded the earth with light and warmth. The trees and grass were a fresher green, the sky a deeper blue. The earth seemed to smile under the peace of God. So the rays of the Sun of Righteousness had penetrated the clouds and darkness of my mind, and dispelled its gloom.

"It seemed to me that everyone must be at peace with God, and animated by His Spirit. Everything that my eyes rested upon seemed to have undergone a change. The trees were more beautiful, and the birds sang more sweetly than ever before; they seemed to be praising the Creator in their songs. I did not care to talk, for fear this happiness might pass away, and I should lose the precious evidence of Jesus' love for me."[1]

The young teenager, of course, was Ellen Harmon, and she related her conversion in *Life Sketches of Ellen G. White.* Is this account in any way typical of adolescent conversion? In trying to understand the spiritual experience of adolescents, we will certainly have to spend some time looking at what conversion is and how it takes place.

We must acknowledge up front that conversion or the new birth is an act of the Holy Spirit ultimately beyond human understanding. In talking to Nicodemus, Jesus compared it to the activity of the wind (John 3:8).

"The wind is heard among the branches of the trees, rustling the leaves and flowers; yet it is invisible, and no man knows whence it comes or whither it goes. So with the work of the Holy Spirit upon the heart. It can no more be explained than can the movements of the wind. A person may not be able to tell the exact time or place, or to trace all the circumstances in the process of conversion; but this does not prove him to be unconverted. By an agency unseen as the wind, Christ is constantly working on the heart. Little by little, perhaps unconsciously to the receiver, impressions are made that tend to draw the soul to Christ. These may be received through meditating upon Him, through reading the Scriptures, or through hearing the word from the living preacher. Suddenly, as the Spirit comes with more direct appeal, the soul gladly surrenders itself to Jesus. By many this is called sudden conversion; but it is the result of long wooing by the Spirit of God—a patient protracted process."[2]

But just because conversion is the Lord's doing, it doesn't follow that it has no human influences. Conversion is related both to personality and internal stresses and to social context. Let's try to examine some of them as we apply the process to the spiritual experience of teenagers.[3]

Understanding Conversion

Students of the subject have debated whether conversion is a rational choice to change beliefs or an emotional explosion quite apart from the individual's will. The term definitely indicates a shift in thinking and behaving, a transformation from one state to another, as in science we speak of the conversion of water to steam. But people have used the term in different ways: (1) a personal commitment to the religion of one's childhood, (2) a switching to another "standard" religion, such as going from Methodist to Pentecostal, or (3) adopting an experimental religion, such as an Eastern religion, Scientology, etc.

Many studies have shown that adolescence is the prime period for conversions. Gillespie cites a number of scholars who maintain that the teen years are the most favorable time for religious conversion.[4] This era is a crucial time for the development of self, as well as being a time of both internal and external conflict.

At the beginning of the 10-year youth retention study, when the participants were 15 and 16 years old, 15 percent indicated that they had experienced a "conversion" to Christ during a specific period while 30 percent claimed that it had been a gradual growth since they were younger. The remaining 55 percent said that it was probably a degree of both.[5] As noted in an earlier chapter, about half of the teens in the NSYR claimed to have had a moving religious experience.

Such a "conversion," then, could be a change that either happens rapidly or is a slower, more gradual process. It could be defined as any process by which a person comes to hold a particular religious commitment regardless of how that process may differ. We generally think of the shift as positive, however—transformations in the life that bring wholeness.

Yet critics have often denounced religion as pathological. Does religion cause people to be emotionally disturbed? Are mentally unbalanced people likely to be attracted to it? Psychologists have noted that religious themes often appear in the babblings of the emotionally disturbed. Once while camping, I met a young man in the "hippie" mode who seriously assured me that he was Jesus Christ. What passes for conversion could be fanaticism.

A number of studies have indicated that recent converts were more likely to have experienced more childhood trauma, unhappy adolescence, and personal stress than the average person. Some have suggested that insecure persons may gravitate to religions that promise certainty as a way of self-control. For example, did seemingly ordinary people join David Koresh in spite of his bizarre views because by offering absolute sureness he provided them with a way of dealing with their latent insecurities?

The type of conversion is also related to the social context in which the individual operates. Some faith groups place a high priority on emotional response. They feature altar calls with mood music, crying, shouting, fainting, and even speaking in tongues. Such groups expect the prospective convert to experience emotional responses as evidence of genuine conversion. I have witnessed youth desperately trying to "get that feeling" while their peers encouraged and prayed with them. The nature of conversion definitely varies with the religious climate in which the youth grew up in. Young people from Pentecostal homes are more likely to talk of being "born again" than are those from Episcopal backgrounds.

As noted above, the mean age for conversions is the mid-teens—the time of Erikson's "identity crisis." The vast majority who join cults do so in their teens or early 20s. Perhaps the crisis of attempting to discover one's identity during adolescence makes one more open to a religion "solution" in order to "find oneself."

People make major life choices during this stage. There is a sense in which a teenager solves or resolves a religious identity crisis that integrates the personality and gives life a new purpose. A key role for those who guide adolescents must be to help them to understand what is essential in conversion and to mentor them through this process.

An attitude is a disposition toward some person or thing. It contains three components—cognitive, affective, and behavioral. Thus it always involves knowing, feeling, and doing something about the object of that attitude. *Faith* can be defined as an attitude. We come to understand something about a religion, to have feelings—positive or negative—toward it, and to take some action. Conversion then is really an attitude change.

Also conversion means that we put a value on the particular religious experience. In the next chapter we will see that one definition of a value is that it is freely chosen. Thus conversion means making a deliberate choice. If a religion is imposed from outside, the individual only appears to hold it. No real conversion has occurred.

However, what about brainwashing and all the cult pressures so prominent during the seventies—sometimes labeled "socially induced conversion"? Well, bombardments of conversion propaganda, combined with isolation of the individual from normal contacts, can lead to information overload, with the result that the prospective convert "snaps" and surrenders the will. The result may be that the worn and highly stressed individual accepts the new belief in order to escape conflict. Instead of conversion we might better label it an example of low sales resistance.

One illustration is an evangelist who visits a prospect three times a day to urge attendance at the nightly meetings and then makes lengthy emotional calls for surrender. Sometimes the evangelist will even come to where the individual is sitting and try to lead him or her to the front. The badgered prospect may find it easier to agree to baptism than to resist the strong sales pitch.

We might also notice this when the minister visits the church school and conducts a baptismal class for, say, the sixth grade, it is very difficult for a given 11-year-old not to go along when all the classmates choose baptism. Neither case represents true conversion. In the youth retention study 18 percent of the midteenagers reported that the reason they were baptized was because they just went along with their parents' religion, and another 9 percent said that the pastor formed a baptismal class and it was expected that everyone would participate. About 40 percent felt that they shouldn't have been baptized at that time.[6]

When we work with adolescents (or even those younger or older), it is unethical to use pressure tactics. We can be satisfied only with genuine choice.

Conversion Models

Students of the subject, such as Raymond F. Paloutzian, have proposed that we can classify conversion into three models.

Sudden conversion. While the most dramatic, it is probably the least common. The prime example offered is that of the apostle Paul, described in Acts 9. This type centers on an *emotional* experience involving unconscious conflict, anxiety, and lack of self-worth, which all becomes resolved in the moment of surrender. However, even though the actual surrender is sudden, it has a background of struggle. Saul (Paul), impressed with the witness of Stephen, had been fighting the conviction that Jesus really was the Messiah. The Voice said to him: "It is hard for you to kick against the goads" (Acts 26:14, NIV). Ellen Harmon's conversion, described in the opening of this chapter, would also fit into this type. It is evident that she also struggled and agonized before the breakthrough. In these cases we find a sudden crisis of self-realization, as when the prodigal son "came to his senses" (Luke 15:17, NIV).

Unconscious conversion. Sometimes people refer to it as "lifelong" conversion. Young people born in religious homes often cannot remember a time they were not Christians. They cannot recall any dramatic turning point. Theirs is not a sudden decision but a gradual reorientation in response to religious nurture. The emphasis here is on *social learning*. The influence of parents has been strong during the growing-up years. Key factors include the *modeling* of religious behavior by the influential adults in their lives and the *reinforcement* of religious expressions made by the youth.

Gradual conversion. This model lies between the other two. It involves a time of growth that eventuates in a choice to embrace the religion. In contrast to emotions or social learning being the primary dynamic, gradual conversion is more *intellectual*. The prospect studies religious material, asks questions, seeks answers, and makes a deliberate decision.

It is important to note that genuine conversion might take any of these paths. No youth should be pressured into a particular type of experience as evidence that the new birth has occurred. Parents, teachers, and leaders should support adolescents in any process that results in a new life in Christ. Results, not process, are what counts.

Gillespie surveyed students in his classes to determine what the evidence of that new life might be. High on the list were: (1) loving and caring people; (2) people who have a clear concept of themselves and a clear sense of mission; (3) a deep commitment to the gospel; and (4) youth who reflect the nature of Christ. Rarely did theological understandings or biblical knowledge surface on the list of evidences.[7]

Since the time of William James' classic *Varieties of Religious Experience* students of the psychology of religion have been interested in phenomenological descriptions of conversion. Many individuals have recorded their conversion experience. The opening quotation from Ellen Harmon is a good example. Here's another.

"One of your ladies gave me a little black book. She asked me to read it. I laughed at her, too, when she said Jesus would give me power over sin. But that night I started to read this little book that says on the cover, *San Juan*. I like this name 'John.' I read two chapters. I read how Jesus made water into wine, and I asked Him if He could change my heart.

The Complex Religion of Teens

"Mr. Wilkerson, something happened that night. Ever since, this block has been different. The piles of garbage still smell just as bad, the roaches in our apartments are just as thick, but in some way everything has changed. I have something inside me now that tells me God is with me, and He will be with me anywhere. I have many problems, but Jesus has changed the biggest problem of all. He has shown me how to live with myself."[8]

Experiences such as those of Rosa and Ellen show us that while conversion is an intensely personal encounter, the common element is a changed life. Themes that often appear in phenomenological descriptions are rapid growth, unification of a divided self, a central focus in life, a change of direction, an act of surrender, and a sense of meaning and purpose. But we all know that a new birth is not a once-for-all-time event. We need a fresh rebirth every day. So how can we help our teenagers maintain their conversion experience?

First of all, we can help them realize that they can repeat the conversion experience by engaging in Bible study, prayer, and meditation. We need to demonstrate to them how to make these things personal in their lives. But there is also the psychological process of *consistency*.

This means that when people have made a public commitment, they do not want to go back on it and face the embarrassment of not following through on what they proclaimed. *Cognitive dissonance* is the uncomfortable tension that comes when our actions do not harmonize with what we have espoused. When a youth has a conversion experience, it is helpful to encourage that teenager to witness to the event before peers. All of us, adolescents included, need to confess Christ publicly. It brings stability to the experience.

In addition to individual factors, group influences can help adolescents maintain their resolve to live the Christian life. Every group creates pressures for conformity and obedience and frowns upon deviance. A group can satisfy such psychological needs of its members as that of belonging, love, support, and closeness. That is why the most effective youth ministry takes place within affirmative peer groups. Adolescents need the support of their fellow teenagers. Our energies are well spent in helping to create a "conversion climate" in our youth fellowship groups.

A youth leader can experience no greater thrill than to share in singing, praying, studying, and witnessing together with teenagers who have found that brand-new life in Jesus Christ.

---

[1] Ellen G. White, *Life Sketches of Ellen G. White* (Mountain View, Calif.: Pacific Press Pub. Assn., 1915), pp. 23, 24.

[2] White, *The Desire of Ages,* p. 172.

[3] I have drawn much of the information in the next two sections from Raymond F. Paloutzian, *Invitation to the Psychology of Religion* (Glenview, Ill.: Scott, Foresman and Company, 1983).

[4] V. Bailey Gillespie, *The Dynamics of Religious Conversion* (Birmingham, Ala.: Religious Education Press, 1991), pp. 93-109.

[5] Roger L. Dudley and Janet Leigh Kangas, *The World of the Adventist Teenager* (Hagerstown, Md.: Review and Herald Pub. Assn., 1990), p. 109.

[6] *Ibid.,* p. 66.

[7] Gillespie, pp. 214, 215.

[8] David Wilkerson, *Hey, Preach—You're Comin' Through!* (Old Tappan, N.J.: Fleming H. Revell, 1968), pp. 14, 15.

CHAPTER 10

What Really Matters

In an academy senior Bible class I posed the ultimate value question. "If you could have any wish granted, what would you ask for?"

The response from one young woman set me back. "I would like for it to be May 6, graduation day." It was then February.

"Wait a minute," I remonstrated. "You can have anything in the world you want, and you are going to waste that chance to wish away three months of your life when you will soon get to graduate anyway without such a wish?"

"That's right," she replied. "All I want is to get out of here and get on with my life."

Talk about bad choices! And she was a well-liked "normal" girl who had never been in any trouble.

All of us, including teenagers, operate on a system of values. Every day we find ourselves faced with choices, and our values determine how we choose. We adults long to see our youth develop the best values, but how does a value system come into being? Maybe they can get worthwhile values directly from us? Perhaps, but we need to think through how that can happen.

Mention the transmission of values between the generations, and we automatically think of ways by which we can get the young people to believe what we believe and to accept the same standards of behavior that we have found valuable. We want to cry out, "Look, kid, I've lived a long while. Look at these gray hairs. I've sorted it all out and have found the essential wisdom. You don't have to blunder along with trial and error. Just take it from me and save yourself a lot of heartache."

But it simply doesn't work that way. The word "value" means not only a *product* (what we value) but also a *process* (the method by which we arrive at what we value). The process begins in early childhood and continues throughout our entire lives. Constantly we find ourselves assigning relative worth to things or concepts, such as wealth, beauty, power, popularity, happiness, altruism, achievement, freedom, security, adventure, peace of mind, and salvation. We do this not in abstract terms but as these values get called into action in the situations that arise during the course of everyday living.

Such assigning suggests a careful sorting through the available options and a deliberate weighing of respective merits. Values, in other words, do not get passively received—we actively develop them. Louis E. Raths and his associates suggest that the process involves seven necessary steps: (1) choosing freely without any coercion; (2) choosing from among real alternatives; (3) choosing after thoughtful consideration of the consequences of each alternative; (4) prizing and cherishing what we have chosen; (5) being willing to affirm our choice publicly; (6) acting upon our choice; and (7) repeating the action so that it becomes a regular part of our life. Unless these seven criteria are present, we may "mouth" values and even go through the motions of some value behavior, but we do not really have values to which our commitment is so strong and lasting that we will cling to them though the heavens fall.[1]

You will have noticed that we could organize this valuing process under three headings: (1) cognitive or reasoning—choosing; (2) affective or attitudinal—prizing; (3) behavioral or action. Let us briefly examine each area.

The Cognitive Component

The premise here is that principled behavior and faith maturity come in part as a result of careful moral reasoning in which the principles and concepts being considered are chosen and internalized only after having been challenged and having passed the scrutiny of a personal examination. Bluntly put, spiritual development does not take place without critical thinking, as we have discussed in earlier chapters. The first three criteria come under this heading.

Choosing freely. "Choose for yourselves this day whom you will serve" (Joshua 24:15, NIV). Coercion is ruled out. Values cannot be imposed by outside pressures. Suppose we visit an Adventist boarding academy and notice that students fill the seats for chapel service. We might conclude that worship is an important value for these teenagers. But if we discover that the school requires chapel and fines those who do not attend, we cannot be sure that this is a value that will endure after the student leaves the school. Only time will reveal what the young person really regards as worthwhile.

Here I am not discussing the rightness or wrongness of compulsory worship attendance. The school may feel that exposure to spiritual things may lead to personal acceptance of them. It may want to create a corporate culture of worship. And, of course, choice is always limited at any age, because the results from bad choices (no firearms allowed on campus, for example) may be too catastrophic, or because some choices may interfere with the rights or comfort of others.

However, we should not fool ourselves into thinking that compliance with regulations indicates moral behavior. We need to be open with young people about the real reasons behind situations in which we are not willing to offer a choice. Above all, we must recognize that only through free choice, without fear of reprisals, do values really form. The key question is not what will the teenagers do now, but what will they do when they are out on their own.

Choosing from alternatives. Suppose that I go to the ice-cream counter and ask what flavors the store has today. The young woman with the white apron tells me that she is out of everything but vanilla. After pondering the situation for a few moments, I reply: "I'll take vanilla." Would you conclude that vanilla is my favorite ice cream? Hardly!

Where one has no real alternatives, no actual choice can exist. If there is no such thing as bad, you cannot choose to do good. That's why God placed the forbidden tree in the Garden of Eden (Gen. 2; 3). Adam and Eve could not opt for obedience to God as their highest value unless they also had an opportunity to choose disobedience. If they were to become truly principled people, a means of rejecting God's claims needed to be provided. Some people are good simply because they have lacked the opportunity to be bad.

Sometimes what seems to be an alternative is not actually one at all or is so unpalatable that no true choice exists. I cannot really say that I value eating, since the only alternative is starving to death—although I can claim that I value some foods above others. If I tell a child to do what I tell them or receive a beating with a belt, I have not really extended a choice. Once a judge asked a convicted murderer if he would prefer being executed by a firing squad or by hanging. Obviously, such a "choice" cannot demonstrate a value. If all options are grim, no "choice" occurs in the sense that we have been using the word. Youth must have at least one alternative that they consider desirable for any value formation actually to take place.

Choosing after thoughtful consideration of the consequences of each alternative. "Suppose a king is about to go to war against another king. Will he not first sit down and consider whether he is able with ten thousand men to oppose the one coming against him with twenty thousand? If he is not able, he will send a delegation while the other is still a long way off and will ask for terms of peace" (Luke 14:31, 32, NIV).

Even if one has freely made a choice from genuine alternatives, no valuing occurs unless it is an informed decision. Suppose I offer a 4-year-old girl a reward. "Would you like this bright, shiny quarter in my right hand or this dirty, old, crumpled $20 bill in my left hand?" She takes the quarter. What does that prove? Only that she has no understanding of the worth of the alternatives. The choice resulted from ignorance. No genuine values are present.

Under peer pressure a teenage boy decides to take up smoking. He has no comprehension of the consequences. What does he know of lung cancer and emphysema? The boy has never experienced such suffering or observed it at close hand in others. Besides, he thinks such things happen only to old people. Teens tend to think they are immortal. Genuine values are not operating in this choice.

A girl compromises her morals in a moment of passion. She cannot visualize the meaning of an abortion, with its anguish and accompanying guilt. Nor can she comprehend the problems of raising a fatherless child alone or the emptiness of a forced marriage. In both of the above examples their choices do not reveal values as internalized principles, since neither young person made such decisions in full knowledge of the consequences.

These first three criteria, each involving an aspect of choice, represent the cognitive or thinking processes of valuing. They tell us that value education must have a rational foundation. That means that if we are to help adolescents develop a mature faith that will carry them through adult life, we must help them to make decisions wisely and with careful thought. One way to do this is to encourage them to think critically rather just accept whatever they hear from so-called authorities.

Creating a Thinking Climate

The Valuegenesis study included a scale to measure how the youth (grades 6 through 12) who completed the survey perceived the "thinking climate" of their local congregations. The 10-year North American Division youth retention study used the same instrument with college-age youth. It employed a five-point response format that ranged from "not at all true" to "very true." The chart below shows the combined percentages of those who answered either "quite true" or "very true."

I learn a lot	34
Most members want to be challenged to think about religious issues and ideas	35
It challenges my thinking	31
It encourages me to ask questions	28
It expects people to learn and think	40

As a study of the content reveals, this scale seeks perceptions as to whether the church climate encourages reasoning and exploring new ideas rather than just mindless conformity. In other words: Do you have to park your brains to be a good Adventist?

Churches generally get low grades on encouraging thinking, and college-age youth are even more pessimistic than the younger group. And while the survey focused on congregations, we could also apply it to homes and schools. It would be interesting to see how students would rate their college classes, their chapels, and their campus churches, and how teenagers would grade their home environments, especially since in the Valuegenesis study the perception of a thinking climate within the church was an important predictor of high faith maturity, denominational loyalty, and the intention to remain an Adventist by age 40.[2]

The Thinking Church Climate Scale is strongly correlated with the Warm Church Climate Scale (.62) but is an even more important predictor of values and commitment. First, it had a correlation of between .20 and .29 with satisfaction with Adventist standards, endorsement of standards, horizontal faith, frequency of prayer, perceptions of their families as warm and caring, and time spent in intergenerational church contact. Next it showed a correlation of between .30 and .39 with witnessing behaviors, frequency of devotional behaviors, importance of religion, value of service, and intention to remain an Adventist at age 40. Finally, it demonstrated a correlation of between .40 and .49 with Adventism as a life goal, denominational loyalty, vertical faith, and overall faith maturity.

Unfortunately, important as it is to any system of nurture and development, such a climate seems to be scarce. Note that only about a third of the youth saw their congregations as places that respect and foster thinking. The average on this scale, with a high of 5, was only 3.0, and public school students rated their congregations slightly— but not significantly—higher than students in our denominational schools.

Furthermore, the older students were more likely to find the thinking component missing. The scale average declined from 3.3

in the seventh grade to 2.75 in the twelfth. Even more alarming, youth from the five mainline Protestant denominations administered the same scale averaged higher on perceptions of a thinking climate in their congregations at every grade level than did Adventist young people.

Learning to think for oneself is an important part of achieving responsible adulthood. If our young people come to feel that the climate of the congregation or of the Adventist school is antagonistic to that purpose, we will likely lose them. One young man put it this way:

"Church has become very boring, and I attend only because if I don't, my parents get all upset. The religion is fine, but the whole atmosphere of the church will just kill it every time."

The fostering of a thinking climate is essential to faith development, because we cannot really "transmit" values to our youth. In our anxiety about seeing our young people "lose their way" and our compulsion to "do something," we may fool ourselves into believing that we can transfer important values directly from our hearts to theirs. But a value cannot be passed from one person to another. We can aid the younger generation only in understanding the process and acquiring the skills and tools that will make it possible for them to develop their own value systems. Seen in this light, true values, faith commitment, and ethical behavior have much more to do with freedom and choice than they do with obedience and conformity. Indeed, principled behavior must sometimes lead to *dis*obedience, as it did with the apostles and with Christian martyrs through the ages. Such freedom to make choices, however, acts responsibly. It is never anarchy, rebellion, or plain contrariness.

No matter how good or right values may be in themselves, the success of value education and spiritual development lies in helping the youth to have power to do the valuing. To be prepared for responsible adulthood, adolescents and young adults must develop the inner capacity to experience values as real and worthwhile *for themselves*. The need is to produce adults who are "strong to think and to act," who are "masters and not slaves of circumstances," and who "possess breadth of mind, clearness of thought, and the courage of their convictions."[3]

I will never forget my sixth-grade teacher. Most of that year is only a blur after the long passage of time, but she had a favorite expression that still rings in my mind. When she would ask a question (and each of her questions had only one right answer), and the student (sometimes I) would respond with "Well . . . I think . . . ," she would usually snap: "And who gave you permission to think?" Even today the message is clear: "Your job is to learn material and give it back to me on demand. Your personal cogitations are neither needed nor desired. This is school!"

I will allow that it was an extreme case and that most educators are not so blunt. Yet in more subtle ways it is exactly the message that many of the older generation have communicated to the developing minds and morals of the younger one. If we do not really value thinking for one's self, we will not be able to transmit this one value that makes possible the acquisition of all others.

Although the cognitive aspect of value acquisition is absolutely vital, it is not, in itself, sufficient. The affective and behavioral domains must also be present. We'll turn to them in the next chapter.

---

[1] See Louis E. Raths, Merrill Harmin, and Sidney B. Simon, *Values and Teaching* (Columbus, Ohio: Charles E. Merrill, 1966), pp. 27-48.

[2] For a complete report on Valuegenesis research, see Roger L. Dudley with V. Bailey Gillespie, *Valuegenesis: Faith in the Balance.*

[3] Ellen G. White, *Education* (Mountain View, Calif.: Pacific Press Pub. Assn., 1903), p. 18.

CHAPTER 11

To Love and to Do

You may have heard the story about the Boy Scout troop leader who gave an inspiring talk to his charges about the importance of following the Scout tradition of "doing a good deed" for someone every day. After going out in search of someone who needed help, three Scouts reported back to their leader.

"We did our good deed for the day," they chimed. "We helped an old lady across the street."

"Wonderful, boys," the Scoutmaster praised. "But tell me, why did it take three of you to help one person across the street?"

"She didn't want to go."

Those of us with a burden for our youth desire very much to help them "across the street" into a life of mature faith and discipleship. However, we must make sure that is where they want to go. We have seen that building a value system involves a cognitive component—it must result from freely choosing something after thoughtful consideration of its merits. But while necessary, reasoning alone is not sufficient. There must also be an affective component. The individual must be emotionally attached to the belief, concept, or behavior. Let's look at that in a little more depth.

Prizing

The fourth mark of a value (see chapter 10) is *prizing* and *cherishing*. When we value something, we esteem it and hold it dear. We are happy with the choice we have made. "Oh, how I love your law!" wrote the psalmist. "I meditate on it all day long" (Ps. 119:97, NIV). That is why teachers of Bible and religion can never be satisfied with simply imparting Bible information or proving the correctness of doctrinal positions. How the student *feels* about the truth presented is equally as important as knowing the facts.

It is possible to choose freely and thoughtfully and yet not be happy with our choice. We do something we would rather not, as when one selects the least objectionable of several undesirable alternatives. A young person may volunteer for some missionary project, such as going door to door passing out literature, out of a sense of duty despite the fact that the youth is uncomfortable with the assignment and would rather be almost anywhere else. Many Christians are miserable in their faith but hang on out of a sense of guilt or fear of punishment. Such choices cannot be called genuine values.

An excellent biblical illustration is the older brother in the parable Jesus told of the lost son. When the prodigal came home, his brother was angry with the acceptance the wastrel received, and accused the forgiving father: "Look! All these years I've been *slaving* for you and never disobeyed your orders. Yet you never gave me even a young goat so I could celebrate with my friends. But when this son *of yours* who has squandered your property with prostitutes comes home, you kill the fattened calf for him!" (Luke 15:29, 30, NIV).

What an insight of the older son's value system Jesus gives us. Sure, he stayed on the farm like a good boy while his brother lived it up. But he wasn't happy about it. He considered it drudgery. Finding no joy in his father's companionship, he thought his brother was the one really having fun. Although he secretly longed to be out there experiencing the world, he stayed home with an eye on the reward he assumed he would eventually receive. When his father died, he would get it all. And now was this lowlife to be cut back in? Was he to eat his cake and have it too? The older brother made a choice, but he didn't value it. Genuine values must be rejoiced in, prized, cherished, and celebrated.

The fifth criterion of a value states that we not only prize our choices but are willing to *affirm them publicly*. When we really value something, we are proud of it. We don't try to hide it, nor does it embarrass us. "If anyone is ashamed of me and my words, the Son of Man will be ashamed of [him or her] when he comes in his glory" (Luke 9:26, NIV). A "secret Christian" is a contradiction in terms— a true oxymoron.

An old story tells about a young new believer who spent a summer working in a northern logging camp. When he returned, a friend asked how he, as a Christian, had gotten along among the rough and profane men in that isolated setting. "Didn't they make fun of you?"

"It was no problem," he answered. "They never found out that I was a Christian."

I recommend that when an adolescent accepts Jesus as personal Savior, we provide opportunity to let that new convert face a peer group and share his or her testimony as soon as possible. "Gang, Mary has something she wants to tell you." "Something exciting has happened, and Fred is thrilled about it."

If I really value something, I want you to know. I may be tactful so as not to come on as pushy, but I look for ways to share with you what is so important to me. Part of God's plan for our salvation is that "you confess with your mouth, 'Jesus is Lord'" (Rom. 10:9, NIV). A value-affirming theme may well be: "I'll tell the world that I'm a Christian."

The Joy-filled Life

Let's pause here and consider how we might encourage adolescents to cherish their spiritual values. A wise man once said that there are three rules for raising children: (1) example, (2) example, (3) and example. When teenagers see the adults who are important in their world living the joy-filled life, they begin to recognize that what their elders have is worthwhile.

It is impossible to emphasize too much the importance of appropriate adult models in the development of faith. Of course, such a thing cannot be just a mindless copying—critical thinking remains crucial. Yet we cannot choose that of which we are unaware. The point is well made that even though imitation alone will not result in true values, observing a model aids the adolescent to see what that value is actually like in practice, and thus makes it possible to choose that value thoughtfully and freely.[1]

I like to think of value transmission as a huge smorgasbord that displays all the tempting dishes of competing values. Here the youth will eventually get to select the items most appealing to them. And which will they choose? Those that are the most colorful and attractive, most delectable, most tasty! It is not our responsibility to force our values upon our young people. But it *is* our responsibility to model our values so attractively that youth cannot help seeing that they are vastly superior to the competition and will then freely choose them for their own systems.

Such modeling works best when set in the framework of the relationships we discussed earlier. What do our youth see in us that indicates that religion means living in relationship with God? Admittedly it is difficult to model the vertical relationship because of its private nature. But let us attempt a brief description.

Such adults live a life of basic trust. They "know that in all things God works for the good of those who love him" (Rom. 8:28, NIV). Therefore, they are not anxious about where the money will come from to pay the bills or about their health or their jobs or their futures. Not that they let things slide. They are responsible and conscientious. But having done their best, they are willing to leave the results with God. While they have their share of life's problems, they do not complain. Rather, they often express their gratitude for God's gracious gifts.

Those modeling such behavior make it clear that they are not earning their own salvation. They do not portray the Christian life as a series of duties that they must accomplish through stern perseverance. Neither do they picture it as a list of prohibitions that they must shun by sheer willpower. None of them go about moaning about their inability to measure up. While they confess that they are sinners, they are not paralyzed with guilt, for they have committed their salvation to Jesus Christ. Rather they believe that He has forgiven their sins and that they are clothed with the robe of His righteousness. Daily they invite the Holy Spirit to control their lives, and they believe that God is working out His character in them.

Their Christian walk, then, is not in long-faced solemnity but in joy. They freely choose the life of faith—they prize and cherish it and live it out. Happily they share their experience with others, and they do so, not like a high-pressure salesman overpowering a customer, but simply and naturally in the course of their daily living.

The opportunities to demonstrate horizontal relationships are much greater, for they occur in every interaction with our fellow humans and, indeed, testify to our walk with God. "Everyone will know that you are my disciples, if you have love for one another" (John 13:35, NRSV).

We model the second greatest commandment by treating all humans (especially our teenagers) with the utmost respect in such a way as to uphold always their sense of dignity and self-worth. Taking them seriously, we listen to them and solicit their input. We will not belittle their ideas, and we will have concern for their private lives. Never will we discriminate on external characteristics such as ethnicity and gender.

Adults who wish to model this value will not tell jokes that denigrate Blacks, Polish, Italians, Jews, or other ethnic groups. Neither will they find them funny when others tell them. They will not accept such stereotypes as "Blacks are irresponsible," "Latins are lazy," "Germans are ruthless," or "women are illogical," but will insist that each individual be evaluated on his or her unique merits. They will not use or encourage so-called funny statements about the inadequacies of the opposite sex—especially those that make light of the sacred institution of marriage. Nor will they employ humor at the expense of their spouses, and will have no place for mother-in-law jokes.

We also affirm the dignity and worth of people by our tolerance of differences. Adults who wish to transmit this value will not rant and rave against other denominations or religious groups. While they are not apologetic for their own beliefs, they freely allow that others have just as much right to teach and practice theirs. They acknowledge the fact that just because some disagree with them does not make these others inferior or bad. And they know that sincere people may be mistaken and that even insincere people are still important to God.

Also they will respect people who differ with them on politics or economics or church policies. Good role models will not look down on those who have less education or fewer possessions than they do or who hold less-prestigious jobs. They see beyond the outward husk to the kernel of intrinsic worth placed within by creation and potential redemption.

When parents, teachers, and church leaders demonstrate such vertical and horizontal relationships, youth will have an excellent probability of developing abstract-universal values and constructing authentic Christian value systems. They do not simply choose them intellectually, but they will prize them emotionally, realizing that they have found something worth keeping. John Gardner reminded us that young people acquire values not by studying ethical principles, but by emulating ethical models. Youth do not begin by analyzing or listing the attributes they wish to develop. Rather, they identify with people they admire who reveal those characteristics in their daily lives. That is why it is so crucial to provide young people with authentic models.[2]

Acting on Values

If the first set of criteria is concerned with cognitive processes (see the previous chapter) and the second set with emotions and feelings, the third set is behavioral in nature. The sixth distinctive mark of a value is *acting upon choices*. Here is where real values show up. The first five criteria could be present, and yet the whole thing could consist of just talk—head religion! Now comes the time, as they say, to "put your money where your mouth is."

If helping people is part of our value system, we will give of our time and energies to do exactly that. Hurricane Katrina, for example, badly damaged Bass Memorial Academy in Mississippi.

The Complex Religion of Teens

Immediately about 100 students from Andrews University volunteered to go and share. They gave up their Labor Day holiday, raised $250 each for travel expenses, rode all night on cramped buses, and slept on a soggy gym floor at the academy. But they cleaned up debris, partially repaired the roof on the boys' dorm, and fed about 5,000 people. Their values and sense of mission greatly moved me.

If we believe in the church, we will open up our wallets and support its programs with our money. No freeloaders here. If the Christian home is important to us, we will treat our spouses and children with love and kindness. If we affirm the dignity of all humanity, we will work for equal status for all people and will refrain from ethnic slurs and jokes. If we belief that war is a violation of our Christian principles, we will strive for peace. And if we value all life, we will not rejoice at the execution of a criminal, and we will treat animals kindly. How we spend our time, our treasure, and our energies provides an important clue to our value system. People who talk about doing good but never do anything about it only *think* they have values. "Not everyone who says to me, 'Lord, Lord,' will enter the kingdom of heaven, but only the one who does the will of my Father in heaven" (Matt. 7:21, NRSV).

The seventh and final criterion of a value is *repeating the action.* Valuing is not a one-shot effort. The person who gives a large offering to missions following a fervent appeal but who never donates anything thereafter does not hold missions in high value. Real values are manifested not by the occasional good or bad action but by the consistent daily life. Things we truly value show up in our behavior in different situations and at different times. Persistent and pervasive, they establish a pattern in living. We can depend upon the person who has developed a genuine value system.

I must caution again, though, that one can *do* value things without having freely and thoughtfully chosen them and without really prizing them. Real values require all three.

So then our task is to aid our adolescents in developing value systems that will allow them to face the challenges of secular society with firm convictions and to be a blessing to God and the world. I have given suggestions in this and the previous chapter to foster the processes of choosing, prizing, and acting in the framework of relationships to God, self, and our fellow humans. By combining these processes with the content of cosmic, overarching, universal-abstract relational values, we may gain a vision of what and how to transmit our precious values so that adolescents may maximize their spirituality and attain to the full potential that God has planned for them.

---

[1] See L. E. Raths, M. Harmin, and S. B. Simon, *Values and Teaching,* p. 226.
[2] See John W. Gardner, *Self-renewal* (New York: Harper and Row, 1963), p. 124.

CHAPTER 12

Skewered on Standards

I believe in God, but some things get blown away—like earrings, makeup, rock, movies, sex before you're married, dances. You haven't really lived. My religion sometimes makes me feel trapped from all the above."

Just another rebellious teenager? Maybe. But there's an odd twist. This young woman added: "Though I won't follow all the rules, I just love sitting in the church."

If there is one subject that captures the attention of adolescents, it is church standards. The youth may not be too interested in abstract doctrine, but they are really intrigued about the rules of living the Christian lifestyle. Let's try another one.

"I also think the Adventist Church is too legalistic. For example, it's OK to wear wedding rings but not engagement rings. They serve the same basic purpose. Some people say you can't go swimming on Sabbath, but you can wade in the water. Why do there have to be such specific rules and fine lines on which one side is black and the other is white? Doesn't the church know that there are a lot of gray areas? All the laws remind me of the Jews of Jesus' time. You could walk only a certain distance on Sabbath. You couldn't carry anything unless it was pinned to your clothes like a handkerchief. And so on.

"I would prefer to work on my personal relationship with God rather than sit through boring worship services that just turn me off more. I think the Adventist Church has at least most of the correct beliefs, so why can't we just live our lives by those principles rather than legalistic rules?"

This letter from one of our youth correspondents is more typical than you would care to believe. I like several things about this young woman. She is obviously thoughtful, she is articulate, and at the time of her letter she was still with us. But she might not be for long, for she struggles—as do thousands of other Adventist youth—with trying to make personal sense out of our church standards.

Make no mistake: The issue of church standards is crucial in the determination of whether or not we will retain the rising generation in the church. In the widely quoted Valuegenesis study that involved some 12,000 young people in grades 6 to 12, acceptance of Adventist standards was the second most important variable in the entire study in predicting whether or not the youth intended to remain as Adventists by age 40 and the most important in predicting denominational loyalty. Thus it would be unthinkable in a book about the religious experience of adolescents not to include a chapter on behavioral standards.

Now, lest you conclude that all adolescents are up on experience and down on the standards, one male wrote: "The lifestyles and standards of the church should be lifted up." As we will shortly see, many teenagers are supportive of Adventist standards—at least some of them. Our mail has run the gamut from reaffirmation to revolt, as more than 1,500 middle adolescents have commented on the standards and rules of the Adventist Church.

The topic is crucial because, as pointed out in the citation from the Valuegenesis study above, a strong relationship between happiness with the standards and a desire to remain in the church exists. The youth retention study conducted by the Institute of Church Ministry further supports this. The latter project surveyed more than 1,500 youth 15 and 16 years old distributed all across the United States and Canada. Given the chief purpose of this 10-year study, perhaps the most important question was: "I intend to remain an active Adventist when I am on my own." To it 76 percent agreed (56 percent of them strongly), 16 percent were uncertain, and only 8 percent disagreed. Of course, it did not turn out to be that positive, but it describes the general pattern.

We correlated several dozen variables with the future-intentions statement, using various statistical techniques. The highest correlation (.52) was with the item on agreement with Adventist standards. Those teenagers who agree that Adventist standards and rules are quite reasonable are more likely to affirm their intentions to remain Adventists when they are on their own than those who disagree with the standards and find them unreasonable.

Of course, a strong relationship between the two variables does not determine the direction of influence or even prove that one causes the other. But logic would suggest that those who find the standards to their liking would naturally decide to "stay with the ship" while those who are unsatisfied might well be thinking of "going overboard." It challenges the church to discover fresh methods of presenting its standards to the next generation so that they will be perceived as reasonable and beneficial. If we find no way to do that, perhaps we need to reexamine them to see if they really reflect what is essential in Adventist theology.

Teenagers Face Off With the Standards

We asked our teenagers to respond to the statement "Adventist standards/rules are quite reasonable" on a five-point scale, with the following results: strongly disagree, 5 percent; somewhat disagree, 17 percent; neutral, 27 percent; somewhat agree, 29 percent; strongly agree, 22 percent. So we have roughly half in agreement, a fourth in disagreement, and the other fourth ambiguous—not a major rebellion, to be sure, but not a sign that all is well, either.

However, notice that the statement is couched in general terms. Next we asked them whether they agreed or disagreed with nine specific Adventist standards. We have arranged their answers in the table below according to descending order of agreement. In every case but that of jewelry/makeup the wording of the table is identical to that of the questionnaire. In the one exception the questionnaire read "decorative jewelry or excessive makeup."

Standard	Percent Agree	Percent Disagree
Recreational drugs	74	22
Tobacco	74	23
Alcohol	71	24
"Unclean" meats	63	25
Premarital sex	62	25
Jewelry/makeup	40	40
Dancing/discos	35	43
Rock music	32	48
Movie theaters	25	55

The health and temperance ministry people among us will be pleased to note that the most agreement comes on these issues. The majority of Adventist youth still recognize the reasonableness of our position on various chemical substances. Whether their behavior matches their beliefs is another question. Still, the church must be concerned to discover that about a fourth of its teenagers either disagree or are uncertain about its traditional health teachings even though modern science has so strongly confirmed them. The general agreement, however, suggests that these are standards that we can promote among adolescents and be reasonably assured of getting their attention.

Church leaders should also find it alarming that only 62 percent agreed with the Adventist position on premarital sex. It would seem to reflect the inroads of societal changes, often lumped together under the label "the sexual revolution." This finding is not peculiar to this particular study, either. The Valuegenesis study asked whether sex should occur only in marriage, and found 68 percent in agreement. The intergenerational value survey[1] of 247 teenagers along with their parents found that 62 percent agreed with the Adventist position on premarital sex. That survey qualified the statement by saying that "premarital sexual intercourse is not wrong *if two people really love each other.*" The study listed above did not contain the qualifier.

In spite of major defections, however, a majority do agree with the first five items. On the last four items, however, a majority were not in agreement, two fifths or more disagreed, and the survey revealed significant blocks of people who took a neutral position on the issue. Movies, rock music, dancing, and jewelry, in that order, seem to be the "big four" areas lacking a consensus with the stated church position.

Of particular interest is the attitude toward the standard of movie theaters. Here only a fourth agreed with the Adventist position, and, for the first time, a majority disagreed. The earlier intergenerational value survey put the question in a positive format: "It is all right to attend the movies if the pictures are carefully selected." Here 62 percent of the youth agreed with this statement, and only 21 percent disagreed. In addition, about 44 percent of the parents agreed, with only 46 percent in disagreement.[2] In the face of cable TV, videos, DVDs, and campus-approved films, the traditional Adventist stand on movies appears to be a lost cause.

This is not simply a chance finding. It is consistent with other research. For example, notice a similar pattern from the results of Valuegenesis:[3]

Standard	Percent Agree	Percent Disagree
Not use illegal drugs	92	5
Not use tobacco	91	6
Not drink beer or liquor	88	8
Not drink wine	74	16
Not eat "unclean" meats	73	16
Sex should only occur in marriage	68	18
Not wear jewelry	39	42
Not listen to rock music	26	55
Not dance	23	57
Not watch movies in theaters	19	64

An amazing congruence exists between these two completely different studies. The order is nearly identical. And in both cases the latter four are the only ones that do not have majority support.

In each of the studies the church's stand on movie theaters comes out especially badly. With the widespread existence of television, DVDs, and videocassettes (which only 8 percent believed they shouldn't watch), the church must consider whether its historic stand is still desirable or realistic. If it is, then it must mount a massive selling campaign. Given the lack of support from those who will be running the church tomorrow and the anecdotal evidence that most Adventists attend the theater, the present standard seems to be but a joke, as any rule that is widely disregarded becomes.

At any rate, in both studies the drop in endorsement from the five or six standards that have majority support to the "big four" is precipitous. In each of the latter more rejected than accepted, and in all but the case of jewelry (which was fairly evenly divided), the majority in Valuegenesis actually rejected the standards. Does it really make a difference?

Some will no doubt say that they are not character issues and should not be a part of our church standards in the first place. While it is not our purpose either to defend or to attack our traditional guidelines in these areas, they are well known and longstanding as part of what it means to be an Adventist. Therefore, opposition to them may be symbolic of a psychological separation from the church—the hinge upon which swings the future status of a young person as to church retention or abandonment. After all, the research has shown that endorsement of standards has a high correlation with having Adventism as a life goal, frequency of devotional behaviors, denominational loyalty, vertical faith, and intentions to remain an Adventist at age 40.

It is certainly clear that regarding church standards as reasonable and right constitutes part of a package of beliefs and behaviors that indicate that youth will stay with the church and become strong, supporting members. In every case the correlations are positive with desirable attitudes and negative with undesirable ones. Of course, we cannot say which attitudes cause which ones. But the tight relationships suggest areas in which we should be working.

It is also clear that standards are not monolithic. Youth do not just reject or accept standards. Rather they do both. Most accept some aspects and most reject some. This finding provides a rich occasion

The Complex Religion of Teens

for a dialogue—among both adults and youth—about the meaning, purpose, and importance of standards.

Some Suggestions for Presenting Standards

Since how teenagers feel about the standards is so intertwined with their future intentions for remaining in or leaving the church, the issue should challenge our best thinking. It is obvious that preaching or lecturing will not do it. However, teenagers are interested in standards and ready to discuss them at the drop of a hat (much more so than abstract doctrines). As a result, we have the readiness factor going for us. We need dialog and discussion to arrive at some sound conclusions. While I certainly don't have all the answers, let's consider a few points.

Jewelry

Adventists do not wear jewelry. But wait. That is, they don't wear some kinds of jewelry. We rule out rings, earrings, and necklaces. But it's OK to wear pins, cuff links, tie clasps, and wristwatches studded with precious gems. As the young woman quoted previously said, wedding rings are accepted but engagement rings are not although they serve the same basic purpose.

A standard answer has been that a wristwatch has a utilitarian purpose while a ring has none. But a friend showed me a "wrist ring." That's right—a rather large ring with a tiny watch set in it. And it does keep time.

So part of the problem is consistency. Are we confused as to just what the standard should be? The related problem is the weakness of our argument. I've faced this question for a number of years and have concluded that our biblical case in this specific area is weak. The most common text used for opposing jewelry is 1 Timothy 2:9. It doesn't seem to focus on jewelry as such but on general modesty and the impression the Christian makes on nonbelievers. While it does mention gold and pearls, it also includes braided hair and expensive clothing, which nobody condemns. Again the problem of consistency!

It is also easy to pass over the positive references to jewelry in

108

Scripture, such as the gifts of Abraham's servant to Rebekah (see Gen. 24:47-53). The high priests wore God-approved jewelry (gold wires worked into the linen, onyx stones on the ephod, 12 precious stones on the breastplate with pure gold chains, gold bells between the pomegranates around the robe's hem, and a crown of pure gold). In the parable of Ezekiel 16 God shows His love for Israel through His gifts of jewelry. Christ will wear many crowns when He comes; He will place star-studded crowns on the redeemed; and heaven's gates, mansions, and streets will glow with jewels.

Now, I have not provided a detailed study of the jewelry subject, nor do I intend to. I am not defending jewelry, for I would prefer not to see it on Adventists. Some years ago I served as youth ministries director of a very conservative conference. One day a woman member approached me. "You ministers," she began, "like to preach to us that we shouldn't wear a wedding band [strongly stressed in that conference], but *you*"—she jabbed her finger at my chest—"wear tie tacks [I was]. Why is the standard different for you?"

"You have a point," I admitted. "I'll take it off." Afterward I went home, put my collection of cuff links and tie tacks away, and have never worn any since that day maybe 35 years ago.

You'll know that I am not on a mission to defend jewelry when I tell you that I have never worn a wedding band although I have been happily married for 53 years at this writing. The point is that if we wish to influence our adolescents we must be consistent, and we must have sound reasons. We need to dialogue with them to discover how their thinking runs. If our position is sound, we have a basis for a good discussion. But if it is weak, we need to admit it. And it applies to all the other standards, too.

Dancing

Obviously different types of dancing exist. David danced before the Lord in holy joy. Some faith groups employ religious dancing, although it is probably quite rare in Adventism. Our campuses often feature folk dances. I knew members who belonged to a "cloggers" group. At one time Adventist schools enjoyed grand marches, which witty students dubbed "vegetarian dances."

So it's too simplistic simply to condemn dancing as a whole. We need to explore just what elements of dancing might violate Christian principles. Here again, consistency will be crucial.

Some years ago a columnist in the *Adventist Review* answered a question from a reader who asked if it was right to dance romantically with his wife in the privacy of their own home. She wanted to, but her husband wasn't sure. The columnist was a church leader for whom I have the highest respect. He was a very wise man who consistently offered good advice each month. But nobody is perfect, and this time he missed it.

He believed that such dancing was wrong. While most readers disagreed with this assessment, he might have had a point if he had reasoned that the music might remind him of his former life before Christ and thus cause him to backslide. But he didn't go that way. Instead, he wrote that "the artificial stimulation of such dances easily replaces genuine love as motivation to romance. It is also because the erotic excitement and unholy sentimentality of romantic dancing destroys one's capacity for calm communication with God." (To protect the administrator's name, I am not giving the reference.)

The column created an outcry and a tremendous backlash of protest. Jokes sprang up all over. It destroyed all hope of reasoned discussion on the subject of dancing. The implication that an act that stimulated sexual feeling between a married couple would meet God's disapproval was so far out of line with a biblical understanding of sex that it set back chances to dialogue with teenagers about a Christian approach to dancing.

Movies

As the surveys have shown, movies present the biggest problem in the question of standards. Again, consistency is crucial. Sometimes we have given the impression that going to a theater to see a movie is wrong, but if it is shown in an approved place on campus or in church, that is OK. Also, the widespread use of videotapes and videodisks along with television has made location a nonissue.

Taking a stand against all movies may be principled, but it is not effective, since, as the surveys show, the majority of Adventists watch them in one place or another, and thus they simply ignore the old standard. Instead, we are going to have to dialogue with youth about the substance of movies and how they affect our Christian lives. The issue must be decided by the *quality* of the experience involved. Discussion questions might be whether one can avoid bad movies like bad novels while at the same time not rejecting all films and all books; how different types of films affect one physically, mentally, emotionally, and spiritually; and what should be the criteria a Christian would use in selecting entertainment.

When I was teaching an academy senior religion class, I gave an assignment for the students to watch a movie and write a reaction to it. One girl picked a title that was actually shown at a program on campus. It certainly would not be considered a bad movie by most standards. But it had a scene in which one character had completely frustrated the hero and the audience. Finally, his patience gone, the hero punched his antagonist in the face and sent him sprawling. The whole audience, caught up in the action, cheered.

The girl wrote that when everyone cheered, she cheered too. But afterward, as she thought of her reaction, she penned: "What has happened to me that I could cheer about seeing another human being get hit? Where are my Christian values? I began to realize that my reaction did not represent the kind of person that I want to be." Here is the kind of thought process we need to generate.

How can we best help our youth in character development? Not just by condemning movies and walking away while they see them anyway. Rather, if we can watch some together and discuss the moral implications with the adolescents, we may stimulate some serious Christian thinking. I am not prepared to give an "approved list" for viewing. Leaders will have to decide the validity of that. But I have found much moral ground in pictures such as *Mr. Holland's Opus, Schindler's List,* and *The Apostle.* Note too that the lessons may be negative as well as positive. They may tell us what to avoid as well as what to embrace, even as the Bible does.

The Complex Religion of Teens

In all discussion it is important not to fall back simply on codes of behavior as if they were sacred and unchangeable, but to search for principles by which the youth can make their own mature decisions. The above standards afford the opportunity to get into such deep spiritual truths as holiness (justification and sanctification), the state of holy joy, and character building through inner purity. The discussions may also lead into the effect our behavior has on others—one of the highest levels of morality.

We should realize, however, that such an approach has its dangers. We might discover that we have been inconsistent in our application of principles. Or we might even find that we can formulate no good reason for some of our rules. The youth may back us into a corner from which we cannot extricate ourselves without appealing to tradition. As a result we may be compelled to join the youth in rethinking why we do what we do. It is not as comfortable to be a searcher as to be an authority.

And, as a church, we will need to be aware of our own failure to do what we ask of the young people. Although adults criticize the music, movies, and dress of teenagers, they often make exceptions for themselves. Such inconsistencies are apparent to adolescents, who in turn can rationalize their own behavior, citing adult hypocrisy. Many of the young people in our study reflected confusion rather than conflict as they reacted to the standards. Why is a certain practice condemned while another that seems quite similar is OK? We dare not expect more from our youth than we are willing to give ourselves.

Adults and teenagers might discuss together the need for standards. One approach might be to pretend that no standards presently exist and ask the youth to begin from zero with a list they would formulate for their own future offspring. Such discussions must be handled skillfully—asking the young people for both the positive and negative sides for each standard discussed in a nonthreatening and unhurried atmosphere characterized by mutual good will. The pluses and minuses could be listed on a chalkboard as the teenagers themselves mention them. Adults should not attempt to manipulate the discussion toward predetermined ends—a technique of which adolescents are extremely wary.

Perhaps most important, adults can develop a one-to-one relationship with an adolescent—remembering that given the chance, a teenager likes to talk, discuss, confide, and communicate with a person who is really caring and interested. Taking one teenager out alone for french fries and a soft drink, allowing the opportunity for opening up the heart without peers around, is probably more productive than taking a carload to the baseball stadium.

Yes, this approach is risky. But if the attitudes of the teenagers toward the standards of the church really determine how likely they are to remain in its fellowship as they reach adulthood, then it is even more risky *not* to make ourselves vulnerable and open a continuing dialogue. We cannot continue with business as usual, standing by the ancient and unmovable codes, if we wish to have a future for our church. Even if the historical standards turn out to be best after all, they will still have to be re-created by this generation.

---

[1] Roger and Peggy Dudley, "Adventist Values: Flying High?" *Ministry*, April 1985, pp. 4-7.
[2] *Ibid.*, p. 7.
[3] Roger L. Dudley with V. Bailey Gillespie, *Valuegenesis: Faith in the Balance*, p. 148.

CHAPTER 13

"By This Time You Ought to Be Teachers" (Heb. 5:12)

I did not write this book primarily for those who teach in formal educational settings, although I hope many of these friends will read it and benefit from it. Yet in a sense all of us are called to be teachers. If you are in some kind of relationship with a teenager—whether parent, pastor, youth pastor, Pathfinder leader, Sabbath school teacher, congregational leader—you are a teacher. What's more, you teach religion. Maybe not formally, but in all of your interactions you transmit what ultimately counts.

So it would seem appropriate in a book devoted to understanding the religious experience of adolescents that we devote one chapter to considering some of the ways we might be more effective in communicating the values that we hold so dear. I've gleaned a few random thoughts from my many years of teaching and working with teenagers that I'd like to share.

The Challenge

It is often difficult to interest the modern adolescent in studying the Bible, whether at home, in regular school classes, or in a Sabbath school setting. Part of this is inherent in the nature of the adolescent experience that we discussed earlier. Such aspects include:

1. A desire for independence that leads them to reject the values

of authority figures—an aversion to having religion forced upon them.

2. The newfound ability to do critical thinking.
3. The shattering of the Godlike image held of their parents and other spiritual leaders.
4. The discovery that many different belief systems exist, and that the value systems of their parents and their church are not the *only* way.
5. The recognition that many adults who profess religion are not really serious about living out its implications.
6. The need for peer approval and support.

What's the Problem?

The *content* of religious education may aggravate the situation. For example, there may be a tendency to create two different worlds—a "religious" one that existed millennia ago in another part of the world and in another culture, as opposed to a "scientific" or "secular" world, which is the real one in which they live.

The continual repetition of familiar Bible stories from early childhood on may lead youth to feel that they know everything about them and fail to find any fresh insights. As one student said to me: "I know all that stuff about Baby Moses. Why do we have to study that?"

Some teachers also present the Bible as if it had been written directly for the twenty-first century, and fail to discover what it meant to the culture in which it was written and how those understandings can be applied to our contemporary situations.

The *methods* of religious education may also be counterproductive. The authoritarian teacher may present "truth" as something to accept without question, memorize, and repeat back on the examination. When we do not allow or encourage adolescents to think for themselves, it makes them feel small and dependent just at the time their developmental scheme impels them to seek independence.

An unsuccessful and unhappy learning experience may lead to an aversion to Bible study. Once I served at an academy in which two of us religion teachers taught in classrooms next to each other. When the first period grades came out, more than half of my colleague's students received the grade of F. "Why did you give out those marks?" I queried him.

"Well, that's what they earned," he told me. Although a fine Christian man who really cared about students, he didn't recognize that when students receive a failing grade in a subject, they usually don't like that subject very much. All of us tend to gravitate to things positive and avoid things negative. So how can we make Bible study a happy experience?

Beyond Bible Facts

Fresh out of college, head filled with learning, I thought that I was a better-than-average Bible teacher. I carefully covered the material and conscientiously submitted my seventh-to-tenth-grade students to detailed and comprehensive examinations. Among the required objectives were knowing the list of Israelite judges, the kings of Israel and Judah in order, the parables of Jesus, and the journeys of the apostle Paul. A fellow teacher looked at what I was handing out, and exclaimed: "Wow! That's a real college exam."

The students responded well, for students usually try to meet the expectations of their teacher if the relationship is good. Only some years later did I stop and ask myself what good I was really doing. I had confused the teaching of *facts* about the Bible with the *process* of helping students make Scripture a part of their daily lives.

Not that Bible facts are without value. A student must have some intellectual grasp of the terrain as a basis for making personal applications. But by itself biblical literacy is no more effective in determining eternal destiny than a thorough knowledge of chemistry or computer science. The Christian teacher cannot afford to evaluate the success of a Bible course by the ability of the students to reproduce previously learned material on an examination. Something more significant is needed.

First, we should give priority to the *affective* domain in our classroom work. Such questions as How do my students feel about the message of Scripture? and What are they willing to do about it? are more important considerations than How much do they know? Of course, Christianity must have an intellectual basis, but it must also include the emotions and the will. Unless we enlist the affective area, the student will not likely respond with enthusiasm to cognitive endeavors.

Therefore, the first job of the teacher is to make sure that every student finds Bible class a happy and successful experience. No student who puts forth even minimal effort should ever receive a D or an F. As mentioned above, assigning a low grade (however well justified) pretty well assures that the young person will develop an aversion to the Bible. It is more important for the teacher to help teenagers accomplish something in proportion to their abilities and then reflect this success in the evaluations than it is to judge rigidly by some a priori standard. I personally like a list of possible projects from which the student can select. With my senior academy religion classes I would hand out a list. "Do this much for a C (nobody gets lower). If you want a B, do additional from this list or for an A from the next list. You determine your own grade by what you are willing to do according to your time and interests. If you are interested in a project that isn't on the list, talk to me about it, and we'll see if it can be incorporated."

Next, it is vital that young people view religion in terms of relationships (see chapter 8). God is our loving Father, Jesus is our Friend, and other humans are our brothers and sisters. Don't create the concept of legalism. Don't preach at students. And don't pile on guilt.

It is especially important that we make the Bible relevant to contemporary life. We are not simply studying the culture of a Middle Eastern country that existed several millennia ago. Youth come to think of the Bible as "long ago and far away"—only remotely connected to their own experience. The Bible does relate how God worked in behalf of and through people who lived in distant areas and ancient times. But it can be much more than that if the teacher leads the students in discovering the timeless principles in Scripture and helps them apply them in a contemporary context. It is the *trea-sure*—not the *vessel*—that we must emphasize.

A basic starting point for this adventure is a good modern-language version of the Bible. The problem with the beloved King James Version is that people don't talk that way anymore. So it immediately creates two worlds. The Bible world is OK for religious talk, but it doesn't cut it in daily life. While we need sound scholarship, we should be free of archaic language. I like the New International Version. But in recent times gender-inclusive versions have become widespread. For many females today the word "man" does not include them. For this I have relied especially on the New Revised Standard Version. Whatever version you choose (and today we have many choices), the criterion should be that the students hear what God says to Mike and Shari rather than only to Moses and Huldah.

In your classes, avoid questions with only one right answer (who were the two sons of Isaac?). Instead, force students to *think*. Teach them to analyze, evaluate, and apply. Demonstrate how to use biblical principles in making personal decisions. Use assignments that release creativity, such as individual research to present a topic, the writing of original poems or songs (yes, they can), keeping a personal spiritual journal, doing a personal Bible paraphrase, and taking part in witness activities.

Most of all, as a person who teaches Bible, you must model what truly effective religion looks like. Morning by morning before my 7:30 class I knelt and asked God to help me make Him attractive to my students that day. You must first sell yourself as a happy, confident, and purposeful human being before students will seriously consider the values you teach.

Some Strategies

A wide selection of literature is available to suggest strategies to encourage students to think and to make moral applications. I'll share briefly a few from my own experience.

Moral dilemmas. The teacher presents a story or other situation that involves conflict or ambiguity in which what is right or wrong isn't clear-cut or obvious. The situation should be relevant to the teenage experience. Some areas might be sexual behavior, abortion, cheating, law violation, Sabbath activities, hazing, dating, shoplifting, drugs, racial issues, treatment of animals, gender issues, etc. The process generally follows these steps:

1. Present the dilemma in written, oral, or visual form (might be a film).
2. Get students to take a tentative position on what action the characters should take.
3. Have them state their positions and—most important—give the reasons they hold them.
4. If the example does not arouse sufficient disagreement, at times complicate the dilemma by adding other factors, using "What if?" questions.
5. Use probing questions to force clear thinking.
6. Have students summarize the reasons for each possible choice, pick the one they are most comfortable with, and explain their reasoning to the other students. The interchange of ideas will cause some whose thinking has been rather shallow to reconsider their own stance.

Value reasoning. A way of thinking, it calls upon youth to consider such questions as What is the principle behind this regulation? How could this principle be applied in such-and-such a situation? What do we mean when we say this is good—morally? healthwise? reputationwise? What is the difference between a factual claim and a moral judgment? How would you feel about this if you were in the place of the people most directly affected? What would happen if everyone behaved in this way? Employ the Bible and other sources in seeking meaningful answers.

One of the components of value reasoning is the *practical syllogism.* This structure from formal logic consists of three elements. An example is: 1. All human beings deserve to be treated with respect. 2. Juvenile delinquents are human beings. 3. Therefore, juvenile delinquents deserve to be treated with respect. The first element, called the major premise, is always a value principle. The second element, or minor premise, is a factual claim. The third element, or conclusion, is the value judgment.

Logical reasoning here demands that we satisfactorily answer three questions. First, is the value principle acceptable—that is, do all humans deserve respect? We test this principle by several means: the "role exchange" test, the "universal consequences" test, the "new cases" test,[*] and by asking if it derives from another principle, a higher principle—such as the creation of humans in God's own image.

Second, is the factual claim true? Factual claims may be true or false. "My daughter is a rocket scientist" is a factual claim, but it is false. We answer this type of question by collecting evidence. Third, does the conclusion follow logically from the major and the minor premise? A yes answer to the third question makes a valid argument, but the conclusion may still not be sound unless the first two questions also evoke yes answers.

Values clarification. Rather than using questions that have a "right" answer and, therefore, call for memorization in place of thinking, employ ones that help clarify values. If, for example, you knew Christ was coming tomorrow, what would you change about your life? What are some things that happen to you when you watch television? How do you feel about yourself when you do such and such? What do you think about a constitutional amendment forbidding gay marriage?

Often current happenings provide the fodder for careful value discussions. For example, as I write, the news contains much debate about the war in Iraq. Rather than stating their views, teachers might try some questions. What is your position on the war in Iraq? What are the biblical and moral reasons for your position? What circumstances, if any, could justify a nation in waging war against another nation? Is the decision to go to war primarily a political and practical decision, or is it a matter of religious principle? In your opinion, should the church as an official body speak out on this issue? Why? What are you willing to do to support your convictions on war and peace?

Debating both sides of an issue can stimulate value thinking. The teacher might assign the students to a particular view, or the discussion might be spontaneous. For example, consider the following premises:

1. A Christian will obey all laws of government unless a law directly contradicts a law of God.
2. A Christian must decide whether a given law is fair and just. Respectful disobedience may be the more principled behavior in some cases.

Another:

1. The husband is head of the house. While he should consider his wife's opinions, he is the one responsible for the final decision in case of an impasse.
2. The wife is an equal partner in marriage. When a difficult decision arises, the couple should explore the various options until they reach a consensus or solution equally satisfactory to both.

One more:

1. The church is the voice of God on earth. When official committees make a decision or appointed leadership lays plans, the Christian member will yield personal opinion and accept the authority of the church and its leadership.
2. Church members need to think for themselves. When poor decisions or bad plans come from those in leadership, the conscientious Christian will respectfully oppose them.

Adults can ask teenagers to list some of their most important values or to rank them from a prepared list. Then they can be led to look for conflicts between two of their values, between a value and certain attitudes, or between a value and certain behaviors.

As indicated above, though, the most important teaching method is the modeling done by the parent or teacher. Adolescents are watching the significant adults in their lives to see what values they really hold important, how they arrive at them, and how they translate them into daily living. Practice is a hundred times more effective than preaching in helping youth learn to move from principle to behavior.

The Complex Religion of Teens

According to Goethe: "What thou hast inherited from thy fathers, acquire it to make it thine." Parents, teachers, pastors, and youth leaders face no greater challenge than to aid adolescents in this acquiring process so that the worthwhile values of the older generation might truly become the *personal* property of the sons and daughters.

---

* In the role exchange test participants identify those whom the judgment would most adversely affect and then determine if they would accept the consequences were they in that position. The universal test asks the question about any practice: "But what if everybody did that?" The new cases test applies the principle in a value judgment to similar relevant cases. Is the participant willing to apply the principle consistently in all situations?

CHAPTER 14

Closing Thoughts

First of all, let me share a story from my experience as a conference director of youth ministries.

"At another camp meeting I was joined by a team of nine young people from one of our colleges. They conducted all the meetings at the youth tent for the 10-day period. It was truly one of the greatest spiritual occasions that I have ever experienced. Teenagers who usually spent their time out on the grounds talking with friends were in the tent singing, praying, and listening. There were some remarkable conversions. After the evening meetings a large group remained each night and prayed conversationally for up to an hour. The spirit of love and fellowship made me think of Pentecost. God was so close that we could feel His presence.

"The week drew to a glorious close. Now only a few hours remained. Since some of the team members had another appointment, one carload would have to leave early and miss the final meeting. Many of us gathered to say goodbye. We prayed together for a while. Tears flowed freely, for we had all become very close in Christ Jesus.

"Then just before departure, the girls who had to leave early decided to change their clothes. They felt they would be more comfortable driving the long hot distance in their shorts rather than in the dresses that they had been wearing. Stepping into their tents, they soon emerged in traveling attire. After loading the last articles into the car, they drove off.

The Complex Religion of Teens

"But their exit did not escape the view of a woman who happened by. As I stood there fighting to control the tears, she came up to me and said harshly, 'The way those girls are dressed is a shame! They shouldn't let people like that come onto the campgrounds.'

"Turning, I walked away from her without saying a word. After all, how do you explain it to someone who hasn't experienced it? How could I tell her about the hours of prayer together—about the thrill of seeing young people give their hearts to Christ as a result of our joint ministry? How could I let her know that she was criticizing and condemning people *that I loved?*

"I'm not defending the wearing of shorts. Maybe the girls shouldn't have. But to me the lack of love and understanding shown by the older woman was far more serious. Why did she feel that way? No one was trying to make her wear shorts. No one was suggesting that they should be adopted as official campgrounds attire.

"Yet she found this upsetting. She felt it wasn't proper attire. Perhaps she was right. But in her haste to condemn without even attempting to discover the reasons the girls wore them, she revealed that she was so insecure that she could not allow someone else to be wrong."

The story I've just related happened 36 years ago. What the girls did probably wouldn't raise an eyebrow today. But I've told the story just as it was written. I have not put it here to expose the critical spirit of the older woman—may she rest in peace. I've already said enough about her.

No, I have another reason. This story is from the manuscript of my first book: *Why Teenagers Reject Religion and What to Do About It* (1978). It was the best seller of any I have written, and I got responses about it from all over the world. Should you find a copy, hang on to it, because it's long out of print. But if you do and open the book, you will not find that story in it. And here's why.

My book editor deleted the passage, maintaining that it gave the wrong lesson. "Apparently," she wrote, "there were many tears and prayers, but a disregard of God's will." Then she quoted Matthew 7:21: "Not every one that saith unto me, Lord, Lord, shall enter into the kingdom of heaven; but he that doeth the will of my Father which is in heaven" (KJV).

I offered to make changes to keep the story in (although what I had written was accurate). Further, I disavowed the wearing of shorts and put the best light on the woman's motives as being genuinely concerned about the lowering of standards. Then I added this material:

"These girls were not being deliberately immodest or rebellious. In their immaturity they had made a mistake in judgment. Yet I knew some things about the depth of their Christian experience that the passer-by could not know. The girls were not perfect, to be sure. But they deserved patient and loving treatment—not condemnation. We should always seek understanding in love before we criticize. Then if with our widened understanding we still see correction to be necessary, it can be administered in the loving spirit of Christ. Ellen White has written:

"'Of all people in the world, reformers should be the most unselfish, the most kind, the most courteous. . . .

"'As the dew and the still showers fall upon the withering plants, so let words fall gently when seeking to win men [youth] from error. God's plan is first to reach the heart.'"[1]

The editor also rejected the revised version. Now, my purpose is not to cast her in a bad light. She was a sincere Christian woman, very helpful to this fledgling author, and, for the most part, we worked well together. Rather, it is important to check on our own attitudes. Do we feel that being "right" is more important than being loving? Do we have the spirit of Jesus, of whom it was said: "A bruised reed he will not break, and a smoldering wick he will not snuff out" (Matt. 12:20, NIV)?

You may be thinking that the incident is so insignificant that the whole experience is a tempest in a teapot. But the general principle is still valid. Standards may get different emphases over the years, but the lesson is critical. If we want to save our adolescents for Christ and His church, we will have to learn to understand them and love them before we can criticize them and correct them. That's what this book has been about.

The Complex Religion of Teens

One morning as I went into my large church I noticed a teenager come down the aisle and sit a couple of rows in front of me. She wore a short dress with spaghetti straps, leaving her arms and shoulders bare. And she had on earrings. I was tempted to think: *That's not suitable dress for church. It seems so worldly.* But then the minister gave the call for prayer. Clutching her Bible, the girl got up, moved to the front of the church, and knelt for special prayer. Now I prayed: *Thank You, God, that she's here in church—dress or no dress. Here where she can be exposed to Your love.*

In this book I have attempted to probe the adolescent mind in regard to spiritual, religious, and moral thinking. I have tried to push home the point that to truly understand is to love. We cannot judge teenagers by our adult standards and experience. They live in a different world. It isn't easy, but somehow we must enter their world if we are going to be effective in reaching them.

A recent report from two administrators at two of our Adventist colleges states: "Our general sense is that the students . . . are, in fact, as spiritual, and perhaps even more so, than their predecessors. They have simply found different ways to develop and express their spiritual journey. . . ."

"Our students' preferences for expression and experience may, in some cases, be quite different from those of previous generations, and this sometimes makes it difficult for prior generations to see the substance behind their expression. We may be evaluating the religiosity on the outside of the cup while missing the genuine cleansing taking place on the inside (Matt. 23)."

What are some things that adolescents need that we adults may have difficulty understanding?

1. Time to think and daydream—to develop abstract thinking—to question values.
2. Time to scream—we need to love them through the period of turmoil, no matter how trying.
3. Time for privacy—time away from parents.
4. Time to explore their sexuality.
5. Time to form a philosophy of life.

6. Time to consider the claims of Jesus Christ on their lives.

What are some of the things we need as adults as we try to understand and help adolescents?

1. To recognize in ourselves the tendency to be intolerant and threatened by evidences of independence in youth.

2. To understand the effect of rigidity and overcontrol on the need for adolescent independence.

3. To recognize the crucial difference between morals and mores (customs).

4. To understand the key role that modeling plays in making religion attractive to youth.

On this last one, may I relate a life-changing experience that actually did appear in *Why Teenagers Reject Religion.*

I had just begun a new assignment as Bible teacher in a certain academy. In the freshman religion class was a tall boy named Larry who seemed to have a lot of hostility built up inside of him. For the first week or so of class he rarely spoke, but the hard glare on his face and the general message of his body language left no doubt that he was thoroughly disgusted with the proceedings and definitely unhappy to be in my class.

One day early in the semester I went to the school office on some business. As I approached the counter, I noticed that Larry was standing there waiting for service. Without thinking about it, I stood beside him as I awaited my turn to be served. As he looked up and noticed me, he jumped away in a highly exaggerated manner and exclaimed, "Don't you get near me!" Of course I was surprised, since I didn't have a contagious disease, and his actions seemed so entirely unprovoked. I couldn't imagine why it was so necessary for him to keep his distance from me. But I tried to be as calm as possible as I asked, "What's the matter, Larry?"

Glaring at me, he spat out: "I hate religion, and *you're religion!*"

Speechless, I walked away with my head spinning. That weekend we took a group of student leaders on a retreat to the conference camp. The whole time there I wrestled with the meaning of that statement: "You're religion!" It began to dawn on me that religion was not something taught only out of a book, even the Bible. Rather, it was the essence of the life of the teacher. This boy had had some negative experiences with religion somewhere along the line. Now he had come to this academy and been forced to take a course in religion that he wanted no part of. As a teacher I was the representative of religion and everything he didn't like about it.

Realizing that Larry would never accept religion until he accepted me, I determined to win the boy over. It took a lot of patience, but before the semester ended we became great friends. He actually ended up expressing appreciation for the class. I am grateful to him because he taught me one of the most important lessons of my life. You are—I am—religion.

Yes, it's true. As I have worked with many adolescents during the years since, I have tried to remember constantly that I *am* religion to them. If they reject me, they will almost certainly spurn what I profess to stand for. But if they perceive me as kind, loving, accepting, and warm, and if they further recognize that these attributes are the direct result of the personal religion I hold, there is a good chance that they will want to investigate my values further.

Some of the best advice to parents, pastors, and teachers of adolescents can be found in the words of the apostle Paul: "Follow my example as I follow the example of Christ" (1 Cor. 11:1, NIV).

---

[1] Ellen G. White, *The Ministry of Healing* (Mountain View, Calif.: Pacific Press Pub. Assn., 1905), p. 57.

[2] Steve Pawluk and Don Williams, "Point/Counterpoint in the Discussion of Adventist Higher Education," *Spectrum* 33, no. 4 (Fall 2005): 57.